THE BOOK OF
RADICAL
ANSWERS

REAL QUESTIONS from REAL KIDS Just Like You

SONYA RENEE TAYLOR

T0018721

Dial Books for Young Readers

DIAL BOOKS FOR YOUNG READERS
An imprint of Penguin Random House LLC, New York

First published in the United States of America by Dial Books for Young Readers,
an imprint of Penguin Random House LLC, 2023

Text copyright © 2023 by Sonya Renee Taylor
Illustrations copyright © 2023 by Shannon Wright

Visit us online at PenguinRandomHouse.com.

Library of Congress Cataloging-in-Publication Data is available.

Printed in the United States of America

LSCC

ISBN 9780593354834 (pbk)
ISBN 9780593354841 (hc)

1st Printing

Design by Sylvia Bi
Text set in Blauth

TABLE OF CONTENTS

INTRODUCTION

When I was young, I had ten billion questions. I wanted to know everything about everything.

I had questions about my body: "Will I have big boobs because Grandma AND Aunt Julia have them?" I had questions about rules we seemed to have for boys and girls: "Why do we say boys can't cry?" I even had questions about how we were treating the planet: "Why don't we recycle?" The most frustrating thing about having all these questions was that no one ever seemed really excited to answer them. The truth is, sometimes people acted downright annoyed by all my questions.

Luckily, I didn't let adults' irritation with my list of curiosities stop my questions from coming. When they didn't have an answer for me, I went looking for my own. I read books, watched the people around me, and, most importantly, I started taking guesses at answers. I used the information I saw in the world and my **intuition** (that hard-to-describe feeling inside all of us that helps us know what to do), and I came up with ideas. I always double-checked my answers by looking for more information in books, and from adults I trusted. But what I started to realize back then was that I was a smart human who already knew so much about life.

Guess what? So are you, and I hope that after reading this book, you will feel more certain about that.

Today, I have lots of jobs. One of them is writing books like this one, but the most important job I have is the work of spreading the idea of radical self-love. **Radical self-love** is the love we had for ourselves when we landed on this big spinning rock we call earth. And that love is still with us. It is the energy that reminds us that we are already good enough, smart enough, awesome enough just as we are. Radical self-love is here to call our attention to the fact that we have massive knowledge already inside of us to tackle the big issues that may arise as we grow up.

After spending years doubting myself and being uncertain if I was good enough, I began asking the most important question of my life: "How can I learn radical self-love?"

I have spent years exploring the answer to that question and the answer I came up with is . . . you don't have to learn radical self-love! It is already inside of you. You were born with it! However, there are many messages we receive each day from the Internet, television, music, even school and businesses that tell us that we are not good enough, and we should buy something or look like someone else to be loveable and worthy. It takes daily practice to learn how to recognize those messages and tune them out. When we do, we can hear our own radical self-love guidance much more clearly.

I can imagine right now someone is saying, "Hey Sonya, what are some tools we can use to better hear our own radical self-love?" Well, I am glad you asked! In the back of this book are **10 Tools for Radical Self-Love**. These tools will help you avoid believing negative messages about yourself and teach you how to stay connected to your own loving inner guidance. So, if you are reading something in this book that tells you to listen to your radical self-love and you find yourself saying, "Great, but how do I do that?" turn to the back of the book and pick one or two tools to practice. I promise they will help you stay on track.

The Book of Radical Answers was written to help you grapple with real-world issues—and the questions in this book were submitted by kids just like you! They were between the ages of ten and fourteen and mostly from the United States, with a few from other countries as well. Most importantly, these questions came from young people who were brave enough to ask about tough and complex subjects—topics some adults won't even talk about. That bravery is how I know young people have what it takes to grow into brilliant, capable, and thoughtful adults.

Some of you submitted questions that were outside of my experience, and I didn't know enough to try to give an answer. While I think I'm pretty darn smart, I do not know everything. Shocking! Thank goodness I have super smart friends from all walks of life. I recruited some of those smart friends to answer questions they had lots of experience in. Those answers are titled **Ask an Expert**.

There are a couple of promises I want to make you about this book. First, I promise to give you honest answers that remind you of how powerful and full of possibility you are. Second, I promise to share all the ways growing up can be fun, complicated, silly, strange, sometimes difficult, and still wonderful. I won't avoid the hard parts, but I promise to always remind you of the joyful parts. You are phenomenal and can get through this messy but magical life as long as you can access what's inside of you already . . . knowledge and radical self-love.

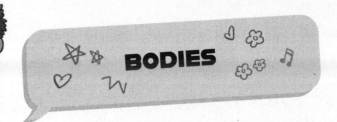

BODIES

What can I say other than if you are reading this book, it's probably a solid guess that you're doing it in a body. That body includes your legs, arms, earlobes, belly, and brain. No, brains are not separate from our bodies, and when I am talking about bodies I am talking about our minds too.

Bodies are one of my favorite subjects and one of the things I most love to talk about! I love it so much, I've written a bazillion books (okay, just four) about our bodies and how learning to love our bodies is a powerful way to create a world of justice and kindness.

Bodies are the BEST! Bodies can also be complex and challenging. They can be funny, smelly, hairy, big, small, and confusing on occasion, but they are without question an incredible gift that allows us humans to participate in this wonky ride of life. Whether you have questions about how your body works, how other people's bodies work, or how to demand boundaries and respect for our bodies, here are some radical answers for you.

Content note: *We will be honestly discussing sexual abuse in this chapter. We want to let you know in advance so you can prepare yourself and take some time out to protect your mental health if needed.*

PUBERTY, PERIODS, AND PENISES

QUESTION: What is puberty?

Puberty seemed to get tons of attention from adults when I was a young person. All my teachers, parents, and the other grown-ups in my life spent a lot of time making puberty seem extra dramatic. When I was upset about pretty much anything, my mother and grandmother would whisper-yell from the kitchen, "You know she's going through puuuuuberrrtyyyyy!" I remember thinking, *Maybe it's puberty, or maybe my mother discussing my bra size aloud with the whole family is just legitimately embarrassing!*

Eventually, I was able to see that puberty didn't have to be a major drama. I came to understand that puberty is a natural part of having a body. **Puberty** describes the age at, or period during which, a young person's body begins to mature and becomes capable of reproducing. The ability to reproduce, i.e., make a baby, is one of the signs that indicates your body has begun to move from childhood into adulthood. This process happens over several years. It involves changes so small you may not even notice, as well as some major shifts in your body, which can include growing taller, voice changes, weight gain, hair growth, breast development, and emotional changes.

We won't cover all the details of puberty in this book because there are tons of great books that talk about the specifics (I even wrote one already! It's called *Celebrate Your Body (and Its Changes, Too!)*). But what I want you to really get is that puberty is not a high-drama event at all. Instead, puberty is all about you becoming a wiser, usually bigger, more mature version of yourself. And I for one think that is pretty cool.

QUESTION: What is a period and why do we call it that?

Hello, a period is the end of a sentence! We all learned that in English class!

Okay, okay, I know you don't mean that kind of period. And I'm glad because I was awful at grammar in school. I believe you're talking about that other kind of period, the one that involves eggs, blood, and monthly cycles, right?

Let me start from the beginning. A **period** is the term many people use to informally describe the bodily experience of menstruation. Over the course of about twenty-eight days, people who have a uterus build up a lining of tissue and blood in their uterus. This lining is meant to nourish a potentially fertilized egg. If that fertilized egg attaches to the uterine wall and grows, it will become a human. If the egg goes unfertilized, the body releases the lining of tissue and blood through the vagina over the course of three to seven days.

This release of what looks like mostly blood happens about once a month and we call it a period. Folks started calling it a period because it happens periodically, or over a period of time each month. The cycle from the day someone first sees blood until they see blood again the next month is a full **menstrual cycle**. Most people see the period as just the time when blood is visible. However, the menstrual cycle is happening all month long inside the body.

For a more detailed conversation about how periods and the menstrual cycle work, there are some great books and online resources. If you want more on the nitty-gritty details of puberty, periods, and reproduction, visit one of my favorite websites for all things bodies and growing up: www.amaze.org. They are amaze-ing!

QUESTION: When will I get my period, and what is the best age to start learning about it?

Story time! My family's summertime trips to the amusement park were a guaranteed delight between June and September when I was a kid. I would wake up at the crack of dawn on the days I knew we were going, and it always seemed like those days were the ones where my mother took the absolute longest time in all of life to get ready so we could leave the house.

She would be infuriatingly slow. Slow like she was trying to torture me. But eventually she would finish getting dressed and we would hop in the car and get to the park. Once I rode that first ride, I would forget all about how outrageously long it took my mother to get dressed and ready to go.

I say all of that to say, your period can be like a mom who takes a long time to get dressed. Or it can be like a younger sibling barging into your room without knocking. Both can be a bit annoying and out of your control. Bodies are smart and they operate on their own natural clock, ensuring our bodily changes happen on the schedule that is best for us as individuals. Your period's arrival depends on your brilliant body's divine timing. In general, a person's period usually arrives about two and a half years after they begin breast development and about six months after they notice **vaginal discharge**, fluid or mucus that keeps a vagina clean and moist and protects it from infection. It is normally white or clear and has minimal smell. The average age of menstruation is around twelve years old but can come as early as eight and as late as fifteen years old.

This is all to say that there is never a bad age to start learning about your body. If you have questions today, then today is a great day to start asking!

> **QUESTION:** What is menopause and how old do you have to be to get it?

No, menopause is not when the teacher tells all the guys in class to stop talking and stand still (men-o-pause, get it?).

Bad dad-jokes aside, **menopause** is the time of life when a body that has experienced menstruation (psst . . . that whole thing I just talked about in the question above, a.k.a. a period) stops menstruating. If menstruation marks the period when a body can make a baby, menopause describes the period of time when the body can no longer make a baby. While menopause is not a part of puberty, it is part of the reproductive journey, and that journey begins in puberty.

It is hard to say exactly how old a person will be when they enter menopause because bodies are complex, and everyone's body is different. There are some bodies that never menstruate, while there are others that begin and stop suddenly for various medical reasons. In general, most menstruating people will enter menopause between forty-five and fifty-five years old. However, people can go into "early" or "premature" menopause. "Early" menopause happens before forty-five and "premature" menopause occurs before forty years old. Various medical conditions can impact when menopause begins. You may have adults in your life that are going through menopause now. It is just another reminder that our bodies continue to change throughout our lives.

QUESTION: How big will my penis grow?

I have no idea! That is a conversation between you and your penis, but I can tell you that whatever size it is, that is the right size for you. There are tons of myths floating around about penises and they often make it seem as if there is such a thing as a perfect-sized penis. Some of those myths make it seem like bigger penises are better than smaller penises, which I personally think is silly. That would be like thinking that a bigger elbow is a perfect-sized elbow. Hey, all elbows are good elbows. Movies, television, and **pornography** can make it seem like having a large penis is what makes someone "manly" or better at sex. Again, all of these are myths, and it is important that we separate the myths from the facts.

Here are a few facts: The first is that penises change size. An erect penis, or a penis that is hard because of blood flowing to it, will be bigger than a flaccid or soft penis. The blood flow to that area causes the penis to stiffen and grow larger and longer. How large and how long depends on a few factors, but the biggest factor is **genes**.

Yup, genes, and not the denim kind. Basically, our bodies already have a map for how tall, wide, hairy, short, light, or dark we will be. These traits are passed down through **biology**. Our bodies will usually look like our birth (or "biological") parents or their birth parents, who look like their parents, and so on. Folks with penises will likely have a similar size penis to the other penises in their biological family.

This is true for you too. On average, erect penises are about six inches in length and soft penises are about three and a half inches in length. And those sizes will vary depending on your unique body. No matter what, I promise your penis will be the perfect size for you!

BODY CARE AND CONCERNS

QUESTION: Are you allowed to touch your own body? I know that you are physically able to, but is it weird to want to understand and touch certain parts of yourself that most people don't see?

I think this is a perfect question for this book of radical answers. Why? Because at the heart of this question is an even bigger, even juicier question that I think every human on the planet should ask. That question is: "Is it okay to get to know myself? I mean really get to know every part of me, inside and out? Even the parts that others can't see?" And here is my answer to that question you didn't even know you were asking me. Drum roll please . . .

YES! IT IS OKAY, NOT WEIRD, TOTALLY AMAZING to want to know every part of yourself inside and out. Look, I believe you should be your most favorite person on the planet. And if that's the case, why wouldn't you want to get to know your most favorite person in every way possible? I want humans to explore every part of themselves because when we know ourselves deeply, we can better care for ourselves. The more information we have, the better choices we make. Having tons of information about our hearts, our minds, and our bodies is going to be a major way we learn to make choices that help us have full, fun, loving lives in these bodies we were assigned to live in.

Now that I have answered that juicy question you didn't ask, let's get into the juicy question you *did* ask: It's absolutely not weird to want to touch your own body! After all, it's yours. And who better to get to know it than you? Every day we have the opportunity to explore new parts of our own sovereign land of which we are the supreme ruler. Of course, we should want to see what grows there, get to know the sights, smells, and textures of it all, because it is ours. I encourage you to touch your body. I encourage you to be a brilliant and brave adventurer who wants to know everything about the magical land that is you.

Here's one key piece of practical advice: Make sure that before you go on your own body safari you wash your hands. You don't want to spread germs across your stunning landscape!

QUESTION: My mom is always bothering me about taking a shower. I don't think it's a big deal. Do I have to shower every day?

How often humans shower or bathe can change based on culture, geography, and even religion. I am not part of the shower security or anything; however, there are some benefits to washing our bodies regularly, which is part of bodily hygiene.

During puberty, your body goes into the full production of **hormones**. These chemicals trigger new reproductive functions in the body. The production of hormones kicks our sweat glands into activation during puberty. These sweat glands live under your armpits, in your groin area (near your genitals), and under your feet. Generally, sweat is an odorless fluid that leaves your body to help it regulate body temperature, but when sweat mixes with the bacteria that naturally lives on your skin, it can create an odor, or what I like to call a case of the funky monkey!

Now, there is nothing wrong with sweating or having a scent to your body, but I believe that part of loving our bodies is also about taking good care of our bodies. Bathing regularly is an example of such care.

Just imagine if your mom cooked your dinner every night but never washed the plate she served your food on. What if instead she just served your next meal on the same plate? Maybe you had spaghetti on Monday and then on Tuesday morning she scooped a helping of cheesy eggs onto the unwashed plate. Later that evening she slapped baked fish on the plate that was coated with caked-on tomato sauce and cheesy-egg residue. Then, in honor of your cousin's birthday, she presented you with a heaping slice of birthday cake . . . but it rested woefully upon the remnants of old spaghetti, cheesy eggs, and a light film of flaky flounder! Ahh . . . yum! (Uh . . . no . . . GROSS.)

I'm pretty sure this is what our clothes must feel like when we go long periods of time without some good old soap and water on our arms, legs, and genitals. Sweat mixed with dark moist places like our armpits or underwear is a recipe for some pretty intense smells. If you are going out in public to participate in school or activities, it is wise to shower, moisturize, brush your teeth, wash your face, and put on deodorant before you go. It is good for your body and for the noses of the people who may smell you. All of this is to say, I am certain your mom wants the best for you, and showers are the best! I encourage you to take one . . . tonight!

QUESTION: I like to stay up late, and my grandmother is always trying to make me go to bed early. How much sleep do I really need?

One of the funniest things about growing up is how much our relationship to sleep changes. When I was in preschool, I HATED nap time! Hated it! I was certain I would miss something important if I allowed my eyelids to rest. Fast-forward a bunch of years later and today I wish I could buy a super size extra large order of naps. I wish I could pass them out during Christmas and shove them in stockings. NAPS ARE THE BEST!

Beyond how I personally feel about sleeping, the truth is, sufficient rest is necessary for young people's brain development. Your brain needs sleep to do all the miraculous functions it will do during and after puberty. This is not just Sonya's opinion either: According to the National Sleep Foundation, young people between the ages of six and thirteen should be getting nine to eleven hours of sleep a day while teens fourteen and up should get eight to ten hours of zzzzz's. Yet according to the CDC (Centers for Disease Control and Prevention), 60 percent of middle schoolers don't get enough sleep, and this number goes up to 70 percent for high schoolers!

As I mentioned earlier, during puberty major changes happen with body and brain development, and sleep is the time when your body can focus all its energy in updating those systems. Think of it like a phone update. You have to shut the whole thing down so the apps run faster. Getting enough sleep is also crucial for maintaining your immune system, your mental health, and your ability to focus in school. Falling asleep can be difficult for many different reasons, but luckily for us, science also says that simply resting is super helpful even if you are awake. So if you can't fall asleep, you can lay your body down and do absolutely nothing. Yup, nothing! In fact, I think you should go rest right now. I'll hold your place in the book. Go on!

QUESTION: Can women have facial hair?

Not only can women have facial hair—most women do! Many **Western countries** (that is, nations that have been strongly culturally, politically, and economically shaped by European values and ideas) have promoted the artificial (and relatively modern) idea that women should be hairless and that they should do a bunch of things to stay that way: shaving, plucking, waxing, laser treatments, and on and on and on. But that idea is rooted in **Eurocentric beauty standards**—centering European bodily features, usually white, Western European—that are damaging and exclusionary, especially to women of color, and even for those white women who naturally have more visible body hair.

In general, humans have the same amount of hair follicles on our bodies as chimpanzees. Human hair is all over our bodies, but sometimes it's less noticeable because it is usually quite thin and fine. Again, this often depends on our **ethnicity** or culture. Different groups of people have different kinds of bodily hair.

Body hair, including armpit hair, helps us control our temperature and attract partners (through how we smell, not how we style our armpit hairs, lol). People who were assigned male at birth (read more about what I mean by this in the Gender section) often have thicker, coarser hair than those who were assigned female, and this is due to hormones. "Male" hormones called androgens increase the production of facial and chest hair. However, anyone with higher levels of androgens in their body will see an increase of hair, not just **cisgender** men.

Although most women have facial hair, there are many reasons why some women may have darker, more visible facial hair. One is that a woman might be **transgender** (again, I'll talk more about gender later on) and have more androgens in her body. Some women also have medical conditions that can lead them to produce more facial hair than is typical.

The development of prominent female facial hair is called **hirsutism**. While hirsutism is a body difference that can impact many women, body activist Harnaam Kaur reminds us that having facial hair does not define our gender or how beautiful we are. In a note she wrote to her younger self she said, "You will grow up to be a gorgeous young woman who will shake the normal societal standards of beauty."

Like Harnaam, there are lots of super cool women in the world with facial hair, reminding us that there are a million ways to be beautiful.

QUESTION: I have a beauty mark on my face and hate everything about how I look. My mom really tries to help me not think negatively about it, but I keep telling her I can't help it. How do I stop hating myself? How can I get past this?

I write a lot about **body shame** in my book *The Body Is Not an Apology,* and one thing I've found is that it starts early. In the book, I write, "For many of us, our first shame memories occur before we even enter our teenage years. It is unsurprising that early on we internalize these negative messages. Being young and particularly impressionable, we take cues from the external world about who we are and who we should be."

Negative messages from the outside world about what it means to be "beautiful" start to chip away at our radical self-love while we're still kids, replacing that self-love with feelings of shame or self-hate, as you mentioned feeling. But did you know that beauty companies *want* you to feel bad about yourself, because they make money when you buy their products to "fix" what's not broken?

I call this system the global **Body Shame Profit Complex.** There are so many industries and companies that depend on you hating yourself, from advertising agencies to plastic surgeons to makeup companies and more. Think about it—if you didn't want to change anything about your looks, would beauty companies be able to make billions of dollars a year? I think not!

All of this leads us to an important question: *Who decides what is beautiful?* Today's beauty ideals might seem like they've been around forever, but that's not true. Our ideas of beauty have always changed across time and space. What was once considered beautiful in certain time periods might be rejected now, and what one culture upholds as beautiful another group might think is a hot mess!

For example, did you know that beauty marks have been highly desirable (thus the very name, "beauty mark") at various times in history? In eighteenth-century Mexico, women would wear fake beauty marks called *chiqueadores* made of fabric or tortoiseshell on their faces to be stylish. They were also popular among aristocrats across Western Europe, where they were called *mouches* in France, and in Hollywood since the early twentieth century! Maybe you don't believe me right now, but your BEAUTY mark is a time-traveling, world-class stunner.

But more importantly—all our rules about beauty are made up! And the current rules tend to uplift an extremely narrow vision of beauty—white, thin, able-bodied, and feminine—and a body type that only about 5 percent of US women naturally possess. One way to stop hating yourself is to remember you are being manipulated into hating yourself. Big greedy companies gave you those negative ideas so they could make you a lifelong customer. Don't let them take advantage of you, my friend! You're not meant to look like anyone except *you*. I'm on team you, not team Body Shame Profit Complex.

If you'd like more info, here are some great websites and social media pages to help you on your journey to take back your power and remember how stunningly beautiful you truly are:

- **www.thebodyisnotanapology.com**
- **www.AdiosBarbie.com**

- **www.centerforbodytrust.com**
- **Follow activists like Stephanie Yeboah and Megan Jayne Crabbe**

QUESTION: Do hormones hurt?

Nope, hormones do not hurt, and boy am I glad because we have lots of them.

Hormones are chemicals in your body that activate certain physical responses to help your body grow and thrive, and different hormone surges control different bodily responses. For example, when someone is about to menstruate, they may have a surge in progesterone, and sometimes those surges can cause symptoms like sore or tender breasts or nipples. Sometimes those surges in hormones can cause emotional sensitivity. But by and large, hormones themselves don't cause us pain.

WEIGHING IN ON WEIGHT

> **QUESTION:** If my doctor tells me I'm overweight, does that mean I'm unhealthy?

This is a big, serious question that is going to require a big, serious answer. First, many of the messages we receive on television, social media, and sometimes even from our families about weight and health are just not true. They are messages left over from outdated science and bias against larger bodies.

For example, one of the ways that doctors currently figure out whether you are "overweight" is by using a tool called **BMI**. BMI stands for **body mass index**, and it was a bad research idea whose beginnings started way back in the 1800s with a social scientist named Adolphe Quetelet. Adolphe invented a system to try to categorize men to figure out what the "average" man should look like. Can you already see how this was a bad idea? There is no specific way all men—much less all people—should look! Quetelet was not a doctor and his system had lots of flaws, including ignoring women and proposing some pretty awful ideas about race.

Then in the 1970s, a researcher named Ancel Keys decided to use Quetelet's system in a research study of 7,500 white men from five different countries to determine who was "overweight." Keys's study again somehow managed to leave out women and people of color (Black, Indigenous, Latine, Middle Eastern, and Asian people). Besides all of that, the tool seemed to be accurate only about 50 percent of the time. If this were a school exam, 50 percent wouldn't even get you a passing grade!

Needless to say, our ideas about weight have been off track and failing for a while. However, we as a society have invested tons of money into BMI, and companies make tons of money off using it, so it is still around. What is most important to know is BMI cannot tell us if someone is healthy or not. There are no shortcuts in determining health.

My friend Deb Burgard has a great YouTube video about what she calls Poodle Science. Dr. Deb tells us it would be silly and ridiculous to assume all dogs should be shaped like poodles, eat what poodles eat, and have their health decided based on how closely they can look like a poodle. A rottweiler will never be built like a poodle, but that doesn't mean the rottweiler is overweight or unhealthy. No, I'm not saying you are a poodle or rottweiler! I am saying loudly to everyone who will listen: "BODY DIFFERENCE IS NATURAL."

The only thing we can know about a person's health by looking at their size is—NOTHING. Size and health are not the same thing, just like poodles and rottweilers are not the same thing. Thinner people can be unhealthy and fatter people can be healthy. The only true way to know someone's health—which, by the way, involves lots of different factors like heart health, mental health, circulatory and nervous system health, plus community and family well-being—and who can assess all of that with a glance?—is for a doctor to do a full exam of all the areas I just mentioned. And when was the last time a doctor asked you about your community?

As you can see, we don't seem to be doing a great job as a society in helping people truly understand and achieve health. But there are some powerful new models that help us get closer. One of those ideas is called **Health at Every Size**, or HAES. It says that our size does not determine our health and that all people of all body types and sizes can practice healthy habits to take care of ourselves. There are also other organizations like National Association to Advance Fat Acceptance (NAAFA), as well as amazing activists like Marilyn Wann and Da'Shaun L. Harrison, who help fat people reclaim the word fat without shame and also ensure fat people are free to live free of **discrimination** and judgment. Because we all deserve that, no matter what size we are.

Lastly, it is important to remember that being "healthy" doesn't make you better than someone who is unhealthy. There are people who, because of illness or disabilities, may never be "healthy," at least not by a doctor's definition. Those people deserve care, respect, and support just as much as anybody with any other kind of body. My friend and amazing fat artist Glen Marla says, "There is no wrong way to have a body." I believe Glen. You should too.

BODY BOUNDARIES

QUESTION: How do I tell my family that I don't like it when they initiate hugging or touching without asking first?

First, I want to say thank you for bringing up this question, because it is so important to learn how to honor our bodies and ask for what we need!

When I was a kid, I was forced to hug all kinds of people I didn't know. It always felt weird. "Sonya, give your aunt Gertrude a hug. Go on!" my mother would say, and then shove me into a strange lady's arms. I knew nothing about Aunt Gertrude except that she wore so much perfume, I felt like I would pass out from the fumes after every awkward squeeze. Not fun!

What you are asking about in this question is boundaries. **Boundaries** are the guidelines for what we will accept and what we will not accept in our lives from other people. Boundaries can be physical, and they can be emotional. But no matter what form they take, boundaries are about choosing for ourselves the conditions that make us feel the safest in our environment and our life.

Having conversations about boundaries with our families can be difficult because we often believe that setting boundaries will hurt people's feelings or make them think we don't like them. None of this is true. But we also cannot control all the reactions that people will have to our boundaries.

Setting good boundaries takes practice. Sometimes it just means getting very comfortable with saying a thing so that it comes out easily. Perhaps you can start with setting boundaries with a friend. You can start by telling a friend, "No, thank you; I do not feel comfortable with a hug." Keep practicing until it's easier to say. And once you feel confident about the words, you can ask your parents or family members to sit down with you for a conversation, and you can tell them how you feel about hugs and touching without **consent**, which is the practice of asking for and receiving permission before you do anything to someone else.

Once you've had this conversation, it is likely that you will have to remind them from time to time and reset your boundaries with them. Boundaries are not easy and take practice. But with practice and patience, it should hopefully get easier.

QUESTION: Why do folks look at me differently as I grow?

Growing is a fascinating process. Have you ever watched a plant grow over time or seen a puppy grow from cute and cuddly furball to huge hairy canine in just a few months? Suddenly, Max the little Labrador is Max-imum size!

Growing can be an exciting time, but sometimes adults forget that it can also be an intense time, and maybe one where kids don't want to feel like they're under a hot spotlight each time someone notices they've gotten taller. I also think that, as you grow, it reminds adults that they're growing older too. And sometimes adults feel worried about getting older. We don't always value older people in our society, just like we don't always respect younger people. This devaluing of—and discriminating against—people based on their age is called **ageism**, and it adds to unfairness and injustice in our society.

Unfortunately, adults who haven't worked through many of their negative ideas about bodies may push those ideas on you as you get older. They may point out the ways your body is different from other young people's bodies. Or they may sexualize your body and talk about how it is developing. It is okay to ask anyone, young or old, not to make comments about your body if it makes you uncomfortable. In the previous question, we talked about setting boundaries and some of the words you can use to ask adults to respect yours. This is an example of asking people, even adults, to honor your emotional boundaries.

A SAFE PLACE FOR OUR BODIES

QUESTION: Do I get to say no to medicine and shots that adults want to put inside my body? I know they think it's best, but what if my gut is screaming no? One time I had a scary allergic reaction to a medication and almost died, so now I feel nervous and want to be in control of my own choices about my body.

You, my friend, have asked a really important but difficult question. Who gets to control our bodies when we're young has become a more complex question as young people have taken leadership in major issues like climate change and gun violence, and as they've begun to demand more respect from the adults around them.

First, I want to acknowledge what feels like maybe the most important part of this question, and that is the part about you feeling nervous because of something that happened in the past. I am super sorry you had a bad reaction to medication and almost died—that must have been terrifying.

Often when we feel like something has gone wrong in the past, we worry that it will go wrong again. You can begin to believe that if you are ever in a similar situation or anything even a little like the past experience, the same terrible outcome will happen. It is normal to feel that way. But just because we have a feeling doesn't mean the feeling is the truth. One of the most important things you will ever learn in life is how to tell the difference between doing something (or not doing something) because of fear or based on your intuition.

If you remember from the opening of the book, our intuition is that sense we have in our stomach when we just *know* something. We may not know how we know, but something in us can feel the right direction to go. Intuition is a hard experience to describe, and it shows up differently for everyone.

Fear, on the other hand, is usually based on having a bad experience in the past and believing other situations will turn out bad too. Sometimes you will have an emotional response to something that isn't based on what is actually happening now. It's based on what has happened or might happen. This is why it is always good to talk these things out with a wise person you trust. They can often help you sort your feelings out.

Here is the truth. You, awesome alive human, did not die. You totally lived. Unless you are writing this question as a ghost, who must be in my house because how else would you have been able to get this question to me? (Yikes—now *I'm* the one who's nervous!) Anyway, my point is, you had a seriously scary situation, and you survived. And hopefully there were some kind adults who helped take care of you after that experience and perhaps tried to make you feel safer.

The role of adults is to keep kids safe and take care of them. This role is not only some natural assignment all mammals have; it is also legally what adults are supposed to do. For this reason, your question gets a bit tricky.

I believe you and all young people should always have a say

about what happens with your body. After all, it's your body! But the adults in your life are responsible for making serious decisions on your behalf. This can be decisions about school, housing, and yes, also medical decisions.

This is partly because adults are expected to have more information about how things may affect you in the long run. Hey, they have been around longer, and that often means they hold a bit more information.

Not only may they have more information, but they can get in trouble legally for not making sure you have the necessary medications for your well-being. Being allergic to one medication does not mean you'll be allergic to them all, and your doctor and medical care team would have taken extra care after your scary allergic reaction to note what additional medications or vaccinations to be careful of.

There's lots of confusing information out in the world about medicines and vaccines, especially due to the COVID-19 pandemic. It can be hard to know what to trust and believe. But I feel pretty certain there are some adults around you who want you to live a long time and are making decisions based on science and what they know about your medical history.

To feel like you have more say in your health decisions, I suggest writing down all the questions you have and all the concerns that come up for you around this topic. Perhaps you can find some time to sit with your doctor and the adults in your life and go through everything on your list. Ask them specific and clear questions and let them know this is part of how you want to build trust and learn more about your own health care. I bet the doctor and nurses will be super impressed with how maturely you are handling it.

At the end of the day, you want to live a long and healthy life. The adults who love you want the same. I believe you all can work together. After all, you're on the same team.

QUESTION: How do I know if I have ADHD?

ASK AN EXPERT: Dr. Loucresie Rupert is a mind doctor. That's my silly way to say she is a psychiatrist, which is a doctor who studies how our minds work. She has spent many years helping all kinds of people, but especially young people, heal from difficult experiences and understand themselves better. Dr. Rupert also lives with ADHD, and all of this made her the perfect person to answer this question.

ADHD, or **attention-deficit/hyperactivity disorder**, is a fancy way to say your brain has trouble controlling when you can concentrate and when you can't. My favorite explanation is that we can certainly concentrate on many things, especially things we like. However, we can't always concentrate on the things we are currently supposed to be doing.

If you:

- **Have trouble paying attention in class**
- **Forget chores, even if you've just been told to do them**

- Can't stop moving
- Interrupt others when they are talking
- Lose things
- Forget to turn in homework
- Have a messy bookbag, room, or locker
- Do things before you can think them through
- Have sensory sensitivities (sensitive to light, texture, noise, touch)
- Can't always tell when someone is annoyed, sad, or making fun of you
- Don't always understand jokes or sayings that other people seem to understand

But:
- Have a great imagination
- Come up with the best ideas
- Think outside the box
- Can work on things you like for hours and hours
- Have lots of energy
- Like to be in charge
- Perform well under pressure

. . . you may have ADHD! You can always make an appointment with a doctor to find out for sure.

People with ADHD can succeed in many areas. We especially do well in fields that require quick and unique problem-solving like scientists, mechanics, construction workers, architects, doctors, lawyers, and nurses. We also do well in creative fields like artists, musicians, writers, designers, and computer coders and programmers.

Having ADHD means your brain works differently, but NOT that your brain works worse than those without ADHD. It's like having an IOS operating system instead of a Windows operating system. Different . . . but not better or worse.

QUESTION: Is it okay for someone to touch your body in a way you're not comfortable with if they're a family member? Could I be misunderstanding that they're showing me they love me? Why do I still feel bad about it but also love them?

I am so proud of you for asking this question, and I am so sorry this is happening to you. Know that I believe you and that you are not alone in experiencing this.

The next thing you need to know is that your body is ALWAYS your own. You get to choose who touches it, and no one should touch you without your consent. It is NEVER acceptable for anyone to touch your body in a way that makes you feel uncomfortable or bad. This is true even if the person is your parent, grandparent, sibling, uncle or aunt, or any other family member.

Read those last two sentences over again. It's NEVER okay for someone to touch you without your consent or in an inappropriate way that makes you feel uncomfortable, INCLUDING your family members. Got it? Okay, good.

Your family members also don't have the right to ask you to touch their body, or anyone else's body, in any way you're uncomfortable with. Many people have experienced a family member inappropriately touching them (or asking to be touched) in a sexual way, like open-mouthed kissing, rubbing their thigh, or touching their breasts and/or genitals with the explanation that it's because the person "loves" them. But this is not what love is. This is sexual abuse, and when it comes from a family member, it's called **incest**.

To learn that what our family member(s) may have told us was "love" is actually abuse can be confusing and scary for a lot of people. After all, we expect that our family members only want the best for us and are there to protect us. And sometimes, because our bodies may have felt physically good during these experiences (even if we didn't want them emotionally), we may think it's okay or not "real" abuse. This is also a common response, but it doesn't change the fact that your family member(s) touching you this way is wrong and it is not your fault.

When someone has been abused by their family member(s), they often continue to love the person or people even while feeling deeply confused, terrified, depressed, and/or angry about what the person did to them. If this has happened to you and/or someone you know, it makes sense that you would feel this way. Since they're your family member(s), you might have happy memories with them, times when they were loving and caring, and you felt completely comfortable. But those times don't erase other times they made you feel unsafe.

Listen to your body (it holds your intuition!) and ask yourself these questions: Does my body tense up when they're around? Who does my body feel at ease with and relaxed around? Your body is trying to tell you who is safe or unsafe, regardless of whether they're a family member. You are allowed to tell that person, "NO! STOP! I don't like that!" when they try to touch you. Not only are you allowed, but you absolutely *should* tell someone if they are touching you in a way that makes you feel unsafe.

The next thing I want to encourage you to do is tell someone else! It doesn't matter if the person who touched you asked you not to or said something bad would happen to you or someone you love. They are lying. You deserve to be safe, and I want you to find an adult you trust who you can talk to about what has been going on, like another relative, a teacher, or a friend's parent. *Keep telling* until someone listens and helps you, because no matter what, you deserve to be safe. If you can't think of who to talk to about this, there are online resources and numbers you can call to get help. Dial or text Childhelp at 1-800-422-4453 or visit the website at www.child-help.org. Remember: Minors cannot, under *any* circumstances, consent to sexual acts with adults, no matter who the adults are.

QUESTION: Why do we even have bodies anyway?

Hmmm. Well . . . let's see . . . because . . . ice cream is good? (If you haven't noticed, I am totally procrastinating.) If you remember the opening of this book, you will know I LOOOOOOVE answering questions. I really do. I love it even when I am completely unsure of the answer. But I've also learned that it's not only okay but a sign of maturity to be able to say "I don't know."

The truth is, *I don't know* why we have bodies. Actually, no one knows for certain. But people have been making some major guesses for thousands of years. Many religions believe we have bodies because the Creator wanted to make humans in his, her, or their own image. Many scientists believe, through the process of evolution, our bodies developed to help us survive life on this planet. I probably believe a combination of both things, plus some other stuff thrown in there, like, we have earlobes because everyone should be able to wear fabulous earrings . . . duh.

Personally, I believe we are much more than just our bodies. We are souls, here to have experiences on Earth, and our bodies help us connect to our souls and have those experiences. Think about all the fun, pleasurable, delicious things you get to experience because you have a body. Is it possible we have bodies just because they allow us to have joy, pleasure, delight, and love while we are on this planet? *I* like that answer. You're welcome to borrow it or think of something enticing on your own.

This is one of those questions I believe each of us has to come up with our own answer to. And I'm certain whatever you come up with will be perfect.

EMOTIONS

Emotions are a big deal! They can be loud, quiet, messy, and hard to figure out. Understanding why we feel the ways we do, and how to communicate those feelings to others in ways that are respectful but honest, is one of the most important things we will ever do in our lives. Accepting and not judging our feelings is something that many grown-ups struggle with. Even we adults forget that we all have more to learn about our emotions, regardless of age.

Puberty can be a time when our emotions are heightened, as our changing hormones can affect how intensely we feel joy, anger, sadness, and the many emotions in between. When I was a young person, there were many days when I felt like an exploding volcano of feelings. Over time I figured out it was possible to feel my emotions without reacting to them. It meant I had to learn to sit with the discomfort, and trust that those big feelings would eventually pass. The more we know about how our emotions are connected to the process of growing up, the more tools we'll have to learn how to regulate our emotions and not get completely swept away by them.

Content note: *This chapter includes an honest discussion about suicide.*

A MESS OF EMOTIONS

QUESTION: Sometimes I'm angry and I don't know why. Is this because of my changing hormones?

Why, Sherlock Holmes, I think you've got it! And you're likely correct. Hormones, those chemicals we begin releasing more of during puberty, can totally give us surges of all kinds of emotions, including anger. Add in figuring out school, friendships, parent expectations, and discovering who you are, all while new hormones course through your veins, and feeling angry and not being sure why seems reasonable to me.

The better we understand our emotions, the more successful we can be at moving through them. Learning how to identify your feelings and make sense of them is a lifelong journey, but there are some tools that can help you get better at it. Most importantly, you need to be able to name what you are feeling. In your question you said that you were feeling angry. I wonder if you got curious about your anger if you would find there are other feelings underneath it.

For example, when I was a kid, I would get angry when my older cousin wouldn't let me go to the movies with her and her friends. Yes, on the surface I was angry, but underneath the anger the actual feeling I was having was loneliness. Sometimes, anger is hiding sadness, fear, shame, worry, and other feelings. A therapist or professional counselor is someone who can help you sort through your feelings by talking about the issues going on in your life. Therapists can be an outstanding way to begin identifying and understanding your feelings. I have been seeing my therapist for more than ten years. (Yes, I know ten years is almost your entire life . . . shush!)

Another powerful way to learn how to manage your emotions is through **meditation**, a practice that helps calm the mind and body by sitting quietly and focusing on the present moment. It is also one of the ten radical self-love tools at the back of this book. Throughout the day our minds can wander everywhere: One minute we're thinking about what happened during lunchtime, and the next we're fretting about how we'll do on an upcoming math test. It's easy to be focused on anything other than the present moment. But usually, the present moment is pretty chill.

Meditation helps us practice coming back to right now, even if right now the dog is barking and your leg is itching. Meditation may sound wildly boring, but I promise it's not. With a little practice, it can help you turn down the volume on those emotions so you can handle them more clearly.

Lastly, journaling is a wonderful way to express and explore your emotions. I've had diaries for most of my life. I write about my biggest joys and greatest disappointments in those pages and they are just for me. Journals are a place to sort through our complicated feelings in private and with as much space as we need. Blank pages won't ground you for talking back to them or stop being your friend for feeling jealous. It is a space where you get to be 100 percent honest with yourself, and that honesty is one of the best ways you can get to know your emotions.

So go get to writing or recording or meditating! Life can be so busy all the time, but when we meditate or journal, we are able to calm our emotions and return to a place of peace.

QUESTION: Why can't we always be happy?

From my point of view there are at least two reasons (probably way more, but I have two) why we can't always be happy. The first is . . . snow. Gosh, I hate snow. So cold and wet!

Okay, ignore snow; the first reason is biology. Humans have emotions. And those emotions are, in part, composed of chemicals in our brain. And those chemicals respond to various experiences and information we receive. Different experiences will activate different chemical centers in our brain, and those chemical centers are not just happiness. They include anger, sadness, and fear. To be fully human is to allow ourselves the full range of human experience, and we are biologically wired to feel a range of emotions.

The second reason is based on philosophy. **Philosophy** is the study of how we understand nature, the world, and ourselves. Different philosophers have different ideas about happiness, but here's mine: If we were happy all the time, how would we know we were happy? In some ways, happiness is an experience we have because we know what unhappiness is.

So if we were always happy, would that emotion still be "happy"? Would we even actually feel it? Get it? No? Me neither . . . I think I broke my own brain on this one.

THE POWER OF GRIEF

> **QUESTION:** My grandma died last summer, and I still can't believe she's gone. How long should grief last? Will I feel sad about it forever?

When my mother died in 2012, I asked myself the very same question. I was devastated, and I worried that I would, indeed, be sad forever.

Over time, I have come to think of grief like giving birth in reverse: When someone is about to give birth, the contractions are more and more intense until the birth happens and then there's a baby and the parent feels love. In grief, often the contractions of sadness are most intense at the very beginning, but the contractions can become less intense over time. All these years later, I still cry sometimes when I think about my mother. But today, I also laugh and roll my eyes at her silly ways and feel grateful that I had her around when I did.

The writer Jamie Anderson once said, "Grief is just love with no place to go." Meaning we may indeed forever feel some sadness about whomever it is that we are grieving. But over time, if we are willing, we can let in other emotions, like joy, and gratitude for the love, and happiness for having someone that we cared so much about. Then, grief becomes not only grief. Hopefully, grief eventually helps us to have a fuller, more beautiful picture of what it means to love someone.

Many people have studied grief over the years. One of those people is psychiatrist Elisabeth Kübler-Ross. In her work, she says we all go through various stages of grief. And one of those stages is anger: We may be angry at the person we are grieving because we feel like they left us. We may be angry because we had no control over the situation, and feeling like we have no control can make us angry sometimes. Perhaps there are unresolved issues from when they were alive.

There are many reasons why we could be angry when a loved one passes away. The most important thing to remember is that anger is a normal part of love and loss. And it's okay to allow ourselves to feel all the feelings that come along with losing someone. If you're feeling angry, reach out to a trusted friend, adult, or counselor, and talk about your feelings. It will help you move through the grief. And hopefully, one day, you'll mostly remember the love.

COMPARISON AND CONFIDENCE

QUESTION: How do you become more self-confident?

Here's the important thing to remember about confidence: It is always changing. Have you ever studied for an exam and felt confident, then got your scores back and yikes, you didn't do as well as you thought you were going to? All at once, your confidence nosedives.

There will be times when we do something incredibly well and we feel a bit more confident, and there are times we feel less confident. Confidence is sometimey (that's what we used to call people who liked you one day and didn't the next). That's why I try not to spend a lot of time on confidence and instead try to focus on radical self-love.

As I write in *The Body Is Not an Apology*, "Radical self-love is deeper, wider, and more expansive than anything we would call self-confidence or self-esteem. It is juicier than self-acceptance. Including the word *radical* offers us a self-love that is the root or origin of our relationship to ourselves. We did not start life in a negative partnership with our bodies . . . We arrived on this planet as LOVE." To get in touch with your radical self-love is to remember that you are already enough, already amazing just as you are, because you EXIST on this planet in this time and space, and that is a sacred celebration!

One of the ways I practice cultivating my self-love is with **affirmations**. These are positive, kind statements we can make about ourselves to help build our radical self-love. I usually make affirmations when I don't feel good or smart enough to succeed at a task.

For example, when I felt like I might not be smart enough to write this book (yes, sometimes I worry about not being smart enough too, even though I have written tons of books!), I wrote affirmations on Post-it Notes that said things like "I have wisdom to share" and "I am smart and capable." I would stick these notes in different places in my house to remind myself each day of how capable I was of writing this book. And I did!

Affirmations helped me make a new story about my abilities, which is tool number four in our radical self-love tools in the back of this book. Practices like affirmations help you remember you don't have to get confidence from any source outside yourself—not from your friends, not from your family, not from your crush or your teachers. You find it within yourself because you are glorious YOU. Living and breathing. Right here, right now. What a gift you are.

QUESTION: Will I ever feel like I fit in? Why is it so hard?

Here's a secret I know from having been a former kid and a current adult: Pretty much everyone has felt like they don't fit in before! Some of us just get good at faking it.

The truth is, we are all fabulously unique. Life would be boring if

42

we were all the same! But for many people, especially when you're younger and just starting to learn about yourself and your place in the world, being the same feels safer than sticking out. This is true even for many adults who are too scared to be their true selves.

I'm sure you've seen and heard both kids and adults who express fear and hatred toward people different from themselves, and who get angry or mean when they don't understand someone else's cultural background, race, gender, sexuality, disability, religion, and more. These are examples of people who haven't gotten in touch with their own radical self-love—their own understanding that everyone is divinely worthy of love and respect just by existing.

Their disconnection manifests in ugly ways, like **racism**, **xenophobia**, **fatphobia**, **homophobia**, **ableism**, **Islamophobia**, **anti-Semitism**, and all the other "isms." But remember this: The goal should never be how you can change yourself to be like everyone else—it should be how we can better value each other for all the different ways we bring wisdom and beauty to this world.

I don't know if you will ever feel like you "fit in." I do know that there are eight billion people on the planet, so you are *definitely* not alone, and there are humans whom you will have things in common with. Look for them online and at school. Find them in characters in books and cool songs. Life is not about fitting in. It is about finding our community and remembering that no matter what we feel like or look like, we will always belong simply because we are *alive*. And everything that is alive is connected to each other. *Not belonging is an illusion. Separation is an illusion. We belong to everything. We belong to each other.*

QUESTION: It's hard being on social media all the time and comparing myself to the people around me—what they have, what they look like, places they get to go, how much attention they get. Does everyone feel like this, or is it just me—and are there healthy ways to manage social media?

Here is a wild thing to consider: Social media didn't always exist. Weird, right? Generations of people older than you didn't have social media at all. I went through my entire teenage years without it. So, this is not something most people have ever had to deal with in the whole history of the world!

Really think about this—there were thousands of years that people weren't comparing each other on Instagram or trying to get more YouTube and TikTok followers. They were just living their lives! I mean, don't get me wrong: People still felt insecure and compared themselves to others before social media. But social media amplifies these feelings of comparison and inadequacy by about seventy gazillion! (Okay, so I made up that number, but it's a lot.) What I really mean is, you are NOT alone in feeling this way.

It's so important to remember that social media platforms are companies that make lots of money off you scrolling all day and comparing yourself to others. Tech companies design phones and apps to be addictive for your brain. Using social media on our phones and tablets and laptops all the time actually changes our brains by making us constantly seek "feel-good" chemicals. We begin to crave the "likes" and judge ourselves based on if we have more or less views, likes, and engagement than our friends and classmates. All of this comparison moves us farther away from our radical self-love. Which is why I suggest taking social media breaks, which can help lessen the temptation to compare ourselves to filtered and staged photos. These kinds of media breaks are part of tool number one in the back of the book, **Dump the Junk**, and they help us remember we are allowed to step away from social media and other messages that do not make us feel powerful and worthy just as we are.

This is easy to forget because social media tends to show you a more filtered "highlight reel" of people's lives rather than an authentic display of all those ups and downs people go through. Think about it. No one has boogers on social media. But EVERYBODY HAS BOOGERS! People often aren't going to post about all their insecurities and the horrible days they had (though some people do, and it can be a good way to find community with others!), and so we get a false sense of what people are really dealing with.

Additionally, lots of people make stuff up on the Internet. Did you know that if you hold a toilet seat up just so, it looks like an airplane window? Folks are pretending to fly on social media when they are really just leaning against a toilet seat! Boy, I sure hope they're clean ones. . . .

Either way, social media is far from a simple reflection of everyday reality. Connect with your real friends, do things that bring you joy, and dump the junk by taking breaks from social media platforms. The more you do these things, the more space you'll have to appreciate your own life instead of wishing you had the shiniest (not necessarily realest) parts of someone else's.

WHEN THINGS GET HARD

QUESTION: Why is it so hard to tell our parents what we actually feel?

Relationships between kids and parents can be one of the most beautiful, but also complicated, relationships we will ever have. Our parents are the first place where we learn what we should expect for care, and love, and guidance. Some of us have parents who have been phenomenal examples of how much care, and love, and guidance to give. Some of us have parents who have not been very good examples. Most of us have parents who have been a little bit of both.

When we are younger, what we most want is to please our parents and to have their approval. And as we get older, we begin to make decisions for ourselves based on our own ideas and beliefs, and those ideas or beliefs may not always be the same as our parents'. This can make it hard to share our thoughts and feelings with our parents, as we may fear their disapproval or worry that we'll upset them, or just fear that they will judge us or not understand.

Part of the work of growing up is learning how to speak our truth to those we love, even if they do not agree or understand. Learning how to honor our experiences and be honest about those experiences with other people in the world, including our parents, is one of the most powerful ways that we can radically love ourselves.

I have been around for more than forty years and it is still a challenge to tell my parent how I feel. Some difficulties are just part of being human. But the braver we are, the easier it gets.

QUESTION: I feel anxious, worried, and nervous all the time about everything. What's wrong with me?

Feeling anxious, worried, and nervous all the time, to the point where it interferes with your daily life, is called **anxiety**. It's a very common mental health condition that comes from experiencing stress and trauma. Many of us, unfortunately, experience a fair amount of stress and trauma throughout our lives. Trauma can come from our families, stress at school, or experiencing BIG events like anxiety over the climate crisis, school shootings, and so many other issues that I cover in this very book. Often we feel anxious when we want to have control over something but are unable to. We might be fearful that if we don't have control, something bad will happen. And we might obsess over all the bad things that could happen to us. Sometimes we even think more bad things are bound to happen to us based on bad things that happened to us in the past.

When you get down to the science of why anxiety exists, it's basically your body trying to keep you safe by alerting you to all the possible dangers around you. Thinking about it like that is a good reminder that as overwhelming and scary as it feels to have anxiety, it's really your body wanting to keep you safe. The key is to help your body learn that those constant alarm bells going off are actually doing more harm than good.

There's nothing "wrong" with you for having anxiety. Instead, the question is how we can find ways to help our bodies know that we're not in constant danger and that it's healthy to relax some-times. We can do this through grounding (not like being sent to your room for the night or being told "No video games for you!" but grounding as in feeling the solid, stable ground beneath you) and other visualization exercises, as well as meditation, therapy, med-ication, and moving our bodies to get the anxiety out of our sys-tems, such as through dancing or swimming. Here's an example: For many years, I had flight anxiety. Every time I got on a plane, my heart began to race and I'd feel terrified. This was a big prob-lem because much of my work required me to fly. I thought I was just being a big scaredy-cat, but it turns out there was more going on than that. I started seeing a therapist for my flight anxiety and eventually realized there were old traumas from my childhood that needed healing, and they were showing up in my fear of flying. At long last, I was able to heal the root cause of the anxiety and feel grounded even when I was in the air.

If your anxiety is a result of something bad actively happen-ing to you, like someone bullying you or committing abuse of any kind against you, stopping the source(s) of the anxiety is crucial! As always, I recommend talking to a trusted adult about your anxiety to find the tools that best work for you. It is possible to reset, feel more centered, and be able to experience your body as a place of safety.

QUESTION: I haven't told anyone this, but sometimes I feel like I don't want to be alive anymore. I'm scared to tell anyone. I don't want them to get scared or mad. But I'm so sad all the time and don't think it's going to get better. What should I do?

First, I want to deeply thank you for asking such an honest question. It can be difficult and scary to share how we feel inside with the people around us, and you just did that, bravely, here. I'm sure all the kids reading this who have similar questions but are too scared to ask are also thanking you right now.

I want you to know that you are not alone in feeling this way: According to a recent study in US high schools, 10 percent of boys and 22 percent of girls had thoughts of **suicide** (wanting to kill themselves) in the previous year. If you feel like you're sad more days than you are happy and it's interfering with your ability to live your daily life, you could have **depression**.

Depression is a mental health condition that can be treated in lots of ways, including therapy and medication. Having depression doesn't automatically mean you are suicidal, but typically when people have thoughts of killing themselves, they also have depression. If you do have depression, you're far from alone. Among adults, according to the National Institute of Mental Health, an estimated *twenty-one million* people in the US had "at least one major depressive episode" in 2020, especially among women, young adults ages eighteen to twenty-five, and mixed-race people.

An important thing to know when it comes to thinking about not wanting to be alive is that *thinking* about it doesn't mean you have to take any action to make it happen. In case this wasn't abundantly clear already, I am definitely a fan of you staying alive! (If there was a fan club devoted to you staying alive, you could say I'd be the fan club president.)

If you think you have depression and/or are suicidal, there are people whose job it is to help us feel safer in this world. I encourage you to talk to a therapist, school counselor, or other trusted adult about how you're feeling. Of course, not everyone feels like they have trusted adults they can talk to about not wanting to be alive. If that describes you, then *I* would like to be an adult you can trust to talk about this, right now. I'm rooting for you to figure out how to live your best life, because creating the life that makes you feel most alive as you get older is a whole lot better than ending your life before you've seen how it all turns out.

Many years ago, I was diagnosed with depression, and I didn't feel like I wanted to live. I even spent some time in the hospital and took medication to help me with those feelings. I am grateful for lots of things in my life, but one of the things I am most grateful for is choosing to get help for my depression and keep living. Life turned out great for me. It took some hard work, but it really did, I promise, and it's because I didn't make a permanent decision based on a temporary feeling.

My friend Kate Bornstein, who is one of the **Ask an Experts** in this book, wrote a whole book about mental health and suicide. It's called *Hello Cruel World: 101 Alternatives to Suicide for Teens, Freaks & Other Outlaws.* Kate's book is guided by the idea that if your life is upsetting you so much that you want to end it, you have the right to do whatever you need to do to make it worth living again, even if other people want you to live a different type of life. The only rule? Don't be mean. That sounds like pretty good advice to me.

I don't know the details of your life and what is making you want to stop living. But I will say it's important for you to consider that as you get older, you will have more control over some of the big things causing you so much pain right now. You won't always be going to school and forced to interact with certain kids in your town or city. You won't even have to stay in that town or city forever! You won't always have to live with your family if you don't want to. You won't always be stopped from doing things you want or expressing yourself as you are because of parental rules.

In 2010, the It Gets Better Project (itgetsbetter.org) was founded to give **LGBTQQIA2S+** (lesbian, gay, bisexual, transgender, queer, questioning, intersex, asexual, **two-spirit**, and more) youth the message that life gets better and is worth living. They showcased millions of LGBTQQIA2S+ adults out there who have grown up to have amazing, fulfilling, better-than-they-could-have-imagined lives. This campaign was a great example in reminding us that the difficulties we are experiencing at any given moment do not have to last forever. Not only does life change, but often, life improves.

Of course, you may be going through things that you are skeptical will get better for you in time, like losing members of your family, or experiencing racism or homophobia or transphobia (or all three), or growing up with no money and worrying how your life will ever change. I'm not going to lie to you (and you're way too smart for that anyway); it's true that those painful things are issues adults find themselves dealing with too, as you can see from the statistics of depressed adults! But I want you to know that even if all the hard and scary things in your life don't "get better," you, my friend, will get wiser, stronger, and, if I have anything to say about it, more in love with the divine miracle of your own existence. Plus, you'll meet new awesome people, go new places, try new foods, listen to new music and movies, and discover new versions of yourself. Your story is just beginning. And your story is worth sticking around for, trust me.

QUESTION: Why do people hurt each other?
I wish we could celebrate each other as we are. I feel sad that things aren't this way in the world. How can we change things to be more loving?

Me too, friend. Me too. The fact that you feel this way means you're a beautiful and kind soul who is in touch with what really matters in this world. Please never lose your tenderness and compassion—it's one of the biggest superpowers on the planet and can only change the world for the better!

This is such an important and big question. One way to understand why people hurt each other is because they are disconnected from their radical self-love. They don't really feel how cherished and already-enough they are because they've grown up in a world that told them otherwise and chipped away at their self-love. Because they never reconnected to their own self-love, they don't extend it to others different from them. So instead, they feel a mix of anger, hatred, fear, and disgust toward anyone they don't understand or who makes them question their own self.

This is a big reason why people become bullies. Another outcome of being disconnected from radical self-love is becoming someone who looks to gain power through greed and hoarding. When we try to find our worth through external things, we create an imbalance where others do not have what they need, and we end up with issues like poverty and violence. A life without radical self-love creates tons of negative outcomes.

When people treat others badly, particularly when they target them with hatred and violence based on their bodies (things like skin color, body size, gender, and more), they engage in what I call "body terrorism." As I write in *The Body Is Not an Apology*, "Dragging ourselves through a lifetime of self-hate endorsed and encouraged by our media and our political and economic systems is a terrifying way to live, and yet millions of people exist in this constant state of fear every day. It is an act of terrorism against our bodies to per-petuate body shame and to support body-based oppression." We see examples of body terrorism in laws that discriminate against LGBTQQIA2S+ youth, in the social obsession with plastic surgery, and in the conditions of self-doubt and shame that have created a mental health crisis.

Once we understand that we're enough just as we are and deserve love and respect, it's easier to extend that same love to oth-ers, including those who are different from us. Once we realize we are all divinely enough, that we ALL deserve to live joyful, safe, and abundant lives, there's no need to fear or hate our fellow humans, or exert control over them. We begin to want joy, safety, resources, and love for everyone because we know we all are safer when everyone has radical self-love. Sympathy and compassion for ourselves lends itself to empathy and compassion for others.

Thankfully, there are a whole bunch of people (myself included, of course!) who realize this and who fight every day for a better future for all people. You can find us protesting for justice for all in the streets, and making art, and writing books, and teaching about inequality, and doing all sorts of other things with our bodies and minds and hearts to help the world be more loving.

This is an invitation to practice tool number nine: **Be in Community**. We are most powerful and effective when we work together toward the change we desire to see. You can help by attending your next local protest, or by joining an organization that fights for what you're most passionate about, or by pursuing a career path that helps people. Here's a cool website if you want to find out how to use your gifts of compassion to help make a better world: www.youthactivismproject.org.

We're so glad you're here, and we're incredibly grateful for all the ways you will help us get to that celebratory loving world you imagine.

SEXUALITY

Two topics that seem to stir up lots of conversation and occasional confusion are sexuality and gender. Conversations about who we are attracted to and how we understand and identify ourselves can be complex and even controversial (which I think is just plain silly. Our identities should not be controversial).

Humans have always expressed their attraction to others and their own gender identities in ways that go beyond the simple idea that boys are boys and girls are girls and people are attracted to the "opposite" sex. Trans (transgender) people have always existed. **Gay** people have always existed. But our societies have not always been accepting of those identities.

Hopefully in this section and the next, we can clear up some confusion about sexuality and gender, and unlock permission to be whoever we are and love whomever we want. We'll also explore your questions about having sex and what it means if you're just not interested in sexual and/or romantic things. (Spoiler alert: It's fine! You are awesome exactly as you are!)

> **QUESTION:** What are the different sexual orientations? How do they work?

There are almost as many different sexual orientations as there are ice cream flavors! (Okay, maybe not that many, but close . . .) The most widely known ones include **heterosexual**, **lesbian**, **gay**, **bisexual**, **pansexual**, and **queer.**

Heterosexual refers to men who have a sexual and/or romantic attraction primarily to women and women who have a sexual and/or romantic attraction primarily to men. Lesbian refers to women who are sexually/romantically attracted mostly to women, while gay usually refers to men who have an attraction for other men. Sometimes women and **non-binary** people (who we will discuss in the Gender section of this book) also use the word gay to describe themselves.

Bisexual traditionally meant a woman or man attracted to both men and women, but as our understandings of gender have branched out to include more types of genders than just women and men, bisexual is now often described as being attracted to two or more genders. Pansexual tends to refer to someone who can experience attraction to people regardless of their gender—think pan- as in the prefix meaning "all," like the supercontinent Pangaea you may have already learned about in school. (If you haven't learned about

Pangaea, look it up!) And queer (which is the term I use to describe my sexual identity) is a sort of umbrella term for people who aren't heterosexual, especially people whose sexual attraction to others includes those not part of the **gender binary**, like non-binary people.

So, for example, a woman who only dates women might call herself lesbian, while another woman who dates women and non-binary people might call herself queer or bisexual. There are also people who experience little to no sexual and/or romantic attraction, known as **asexual** or **aromantic** ("ace" for short); people who experience very limited sexual attraction, known as **greysexual**; and people who experience some sexual attraction, but usually in certain romantic or emotionally attached situations only, known as **demisexual**.

The ways we understand and express our sexualities are always expanding and evolving, so any detailed list we could provide today will likely be out of style in the near future. Consider how the term LGBTQQIA2S+ came about: In the 1950s, social movements for gay equality were focused on men, but after women protested sexism and developed their own groups, the movement started talking about "gay and lesbian" rights in the 1970s and then "gay, lesbian, and bisexual" rights in the '80s and '90s.

But trans women like Marsha P. Johnson and Sylvia Rivera, who led the June 1969 Stonewall Uprising in New York that sparked the modern-day gay rights movement, were being excluded from the conversation about gender and sexuality rights. As more trans people protested and began asking for recognition for how they'd fought for gay equality from the beginning, the language expanded to LGBT in the '90s.

Then, queer, questioning, **intersex** (those born with both male and female biological characteristics), and asexual were added in the late '90s and 2000s. In the mid-2000s the "+" was added to acknowledge that this list will welcome many others as we discover new ways to understand ourselves and find community with others who can relate. As they say, the more the merrier!

QUESTION: Can you tell your sexuality when you're eleven?

Sure you can! Some people's experience of attraction may start very young, while for others it can start when they're older. But first, it's important to remember that not all attraction is sexual attraction. We can be attracted to personalities, someone's sense of style, or somebody's ability to do a perfect cartwheel. That doesn't necessarily mean we are sexually attracted to someone.

Sexual attraction usually occurs around the time that we begin experiencing puberty. Our hormones start to send messages to our brain, and our brain starts to send messages to our genitals that tell us we like people in "that way." We usually describe "that way" as sexual or romantic.

Exactly when our body will start to send those signals is as individual as our own puberty journeys. For some people it happens when they are younger, perhaps nine or ten. For others it can happen when they are a bit older, perhaps fourteen or fifteen. It is also possible that as your body goes through these changes, you'll feel uncertain about whom you're attracted to. Or maybe you'll feel like you might be asexual and/or aromantic, that you're not attracted to anyone, and you don't get all the fuss about exploring sex and/or dating. Hey, that's all totally fine. Your ideas and feelings about your sexuality will continue to get clearer as you grow, and whatever time frame you experience is the perfect timing for your unique body. And so, yes, it is possible to know your sexuality from a young age. And it is also possible that your sexuality will change, like so many things, as you get older.

QUESTION: How do I know if I am gay or bisexual?

Labels are great . . . on occasion. For example: Without them, you might think you're about to eat jam, only to discover you just opened a jar of sardines. (Yuck, not the same thing.) In this case, yay, labels!

However, we can just as easily get stuck trying to label ourselves and everyone else even though humans are often more complicated than that. For instance, you may be gay or you may be bi, and either or neither is fine. What's most important is that you are cool with who you are, even if you haven't figured out a label for all your parts and pieces yet.

Nevertheless, there are questions you can ask yourself that may help you sort out your sexuality. I'd suggest you pay attention to who you find really intriguing and explore what those feelings are: admiration, romantic, sexual, or a combination of the above? (It's okay if you don't immediately know.) Who do you feel a magnetic pull toward? Who do you notice and who falls into the background? If you find your answers lean more to one gender than another, that may give you some clues into which identity you most align with, gay or bi.

Remember, your answers today are not written in concrete and may change over time as you gain more experiences in the world and meet new people, and that's totally fine! Sexual fluidity, or having who we're attracted to shift and change over time, is totally a thing, and has even been studied and written about by researchers.

It makes sense that we want to have ourselves figured out NOW instead of in the future. But remember that we all grow and change, and you don't have to have everything about yourself figured out right now. No sexual orientation is the "right" one, and it's also not more valuable to be gay rather than bi or vice versa. In time, it'll become clearer who you're attracted to, so try not to rush it and enjoy the ride!

QUESTION: I've had crushes on people from many different genders—boys, girls, and my non-binary friend. What does this mean about my sexuality?

This could mean that you're pansexual, if people's gender isn't really a factor for you in who you're attracted to. That is, some people are specifically attracted to certain genders, while for others, gender is more in the background and other things, like individual people's personalities, are the focus. Or "queer" might feel better for you, or another similar term—it's really about what feels right to you.

Also note that many people find themselves more attracted to a specific gender but still experience attraction to other genders. For example, a boy could be mostly attracted to girls but still sometimes be attracted to other boys, and he could identify with the term bisexual even if his attraction isn't split 50/50 between boys and girls. (Who wants to make their sexuality into a math equation anyway?!) However you ultimately identify or understand your sexuality, may the journey you take to get there be filled with awesome and interesting people who are kind and respectful of you! You got this.

> **QUESTION:** If a boy is trans (that is, he was assigned female at birth and then he transitioned), is he gay if he likes a boy or straight if he likes a girl? Should I ask him?

First, trans people's sexuality works the same as it does if they're cis (cisgender, which is a word used to describe people who aren't trans—who continue to identify with the gender they were assigned at birth). If someone identifies as male and is generally attracted to women, they tend to identify as heterosexual. This is true for both trans men and cis men. And if someone is male, whether they're cis or trans, and is generally attracted to men, they tend to identify as gay. But of course, at the end of the day, how this person identifies his sexuality is up to him.

Also, just because someone is attracted to people of the same gender doesn't mean those are the only people they're attracted to. For example, if this boy likes boys, he's not automatically gay—he could also be attracted to girls or non-binary people, which would make him bisexual, queer, pansexual, or any number of other ways to identify. Liking someone one time does not decide our sexual orientation. If you liked apple pie one time, it doesn't mean that is all you shall eat forever! Attraction changes, and there are endless ways we can describe our attraction. Some of them are terms we already know, and some of them are terms we will make up as we go along. Again, how this person identifies is ultimately up to him to decide.

I'm going to answer the last part of your question by asking a few more questions: Is this person your friend? Do you have a close relationship with him? Do you talk about personal subjects like family or crushes with each other? If the answer is yes to all three, then perhaps you can ask him. But you might want to get his consent before you ask such a personal question.

If the answer is no, then, as my mother would say when I would ask her about her conversations with Grandma: "Mind your business." How people identify is a very personal and intimate conversation. And no one owes anyone an explanation about the details of their identity. We all deserve to learn and live without the pressure of having to explain who we are to strangers.

TO DO "IT" OR NOT TO DO "IT"

QUESTION: How do I know when I'm ready to have sex? How do I keep myself safe?

Sex! It was the biggest, most titillating conversation I could have in middle school. Everyone wanted to know who was "doing it" and who they were "doing it" with.

We were nosy! Of course we were. Sex seemed like both a big deal and a bit of a secret based on how television was constantly showing it and how my parents were always covering my eyes during sex scenes in movies. It certainly made me think I was missing out on something mysterious and important.

As an adult, I realized sex can be serious, but it shouldn't be a mystery. Quite simply, the more we know about sex, the better prepared we are to know if we are ready to have it.

Adults in society give young people so many conflicting messages about sex. TV says everyone is having it while teachers, preachers, and parents are saying Don't Do It. It felt confusing to me, and I imagine it might still feel pretty confusing to you. But as I said earlier and as with many situations in life, learning to listen to your intuition is one of your biggest tools when it comes to figuring out if you are ready to have sex.

Firstly, it is important to be clear about what you mean by sex.

People use the term sex to describe everything from sexual inter-course, which is genital penetration, to oral sex and other sexual activities that can include kissing or touching various parts of the body. There is no single definition of sex. You may feel ready to engage in some kinds of sexual acts but not others, and that is okay. You might feel pressured or shamed into having sex, or NOT having sex, by others, but what truly matters is how YOU feel.

And if you're not sure how you feel, it's okay to take time to tap into your own truth. In fact, I highly recommend it! It's also normal to feel unsure for a while, because you haven't done this before. Learn-ing your own comfort level will be super important in understanding what you do or do not feel ready to do.

An equally valuable part of learning to listen to and trust your-self sexually is to learn your own body before you decide to have sex with another person. **Masturbation** helps you get comfortable with how your body works and what feels good to you. Different people will like different things when it comes to being sexual (or not) and knowing what makes your body feel good is a powerful tool in figur-ing out what you are and are not ready for.

By spending time exploring what sensations you do and do not like by yourself before you have sex with someone else, you will be more empowered to speak up and communicate about what works best for you when you are with a partner. After all, our sexual part-ners are not mind readers. We can't know what other people will like in a sexual context until we talk to them about it.

If you do decide you want to explore your sexuality with some-one else, it's crucial to choose someone you feel comfortable around, who you can talk to, and who listens to and RESPECTS you. How will you know someone respects you? Because they will ask you for CONSENT and will honor your sexual BOUNDARIES. Both are sacred and yours and yours alone to decide on.

Consent is the act of asking permission from the other person before doing anything to them; it doesn't matter if they are touching your knee, kissing, or taking off your clothes. Consent is mandatory in any sexual situation. If anyone ever asks you to do something sexual that you aren't comfortable with, and they don't listen when you let them know you're uncomfortable, they are disrespecting your boundaries and they are NOT a safe person to have sex with. Likewise, if you are not ready to honor other people's boundaries and ask for clear consent, then you are also not ready to have sex!

This is true even if you've had sex with them before, and even if you're already in a relationship with them. Sex is a vulnerable and intimate act (after all, you are usually naked). You should only have sex with someone who is willing to be responsible and take your vulnerability seriously. If they can't do that, they don't deserve to be with you.

Finally, remember that if you are not ready to practice safer sex, you may not be ready to have sex. Safer sex refers to precautions you can take when you have sex to make sure that you're protected from **STIs** (sexually transmitted infections) and accidental pregnancy, depending on what you're doing and with whom. For example, you'll need condoms if you're having sex that involves penises, you may need condoms and another form of birth control if you are having sex that involves penises and vaginas, and you'll need items like dental dams for sex involving vulvas.

It is important to learn about the different STIs and how best to prevent becoming infected, as well as how to care for yourself and other partners if you do become infected. Organizations like Planned Parenthood in the US and LGBTQQIA2S+ centers often have condoms, lubrication, and dental dams available for free as well as free or discounted hormonal contraceptives, and there is always a knowledgeable staff person who can answer your questions. If someone doesn't want to help you stay safer during sex, they aren't respecting you and aren't ready to be having sex with anyone—certainly not awesome you.

Having sex can be a big decision and it is best when we are emotionally mature enough to handle all the issues I mentioned above. Talking with a trusted adult who can help you think things through in a loving way is a great idea. Maybe the person who got you this book (if you didn't buy it or check it out yourself) might be a great choice to talk some of this through with.

QUESTION: A bunch of kids in my class watch porn and laugh about it. One day I decided to look at it too. It kind of made me feel weird when I watched it. Is there something wrong with me for watching it? Was that a bad thing to do?

You are not bad or wrong for wanting to know what other kids are talking about and looking at. That is just part of growing up. At the same time, there are a few issues with porn that are important to remember. Porn (short for pornography) is sexually explicit media made for adults. It is illegal to show porn to young people under eighteen. You're still learning about sex and your body, and porn often shows a lot of things that can be confusing and even scary for kids, such as violence and disrespect.

Because porn is about making money, it's usually not an accurate portrayal of what it's like for people to have sex. People's bodies, behaviors, and actions in porn are often not realistic. Remember, like in all movies, the actors are doing a job, and what we do at work is often not what we do with the people we love and care about.

The other thing about porn is that depending on who made the porn movie, the actors are not always treated with respect or justice. Some producers can even be abusive toward the people who star in the porn films, particularly women, trans, and young people. On websites where anyone can upload porn, there is even porn featuring people under eighteen, which is illegal and a form of sexual abuse. As you can see, besides being illegal for youth under eighteen, porn has some serious issues that make it not suitable for young folks.

Having said all of this, most adults have seen porn at some point in their lives. It's not bad to want to learn about sexuality, and it's not bad to have sexual thoughts and feelings. On the contrary—those are important parts of growing up and very common! You just need to be careful to make sure that you're not exposing yourself to content that gives you false ideas and images about sex. There's no need to look at porn to get your sex education when there are phenomenal websites like AMAZE.org.

COMING OUT

QUESTION: How/when do I come out?
How do I know who to trust to come out to?

How and when to come out is a very personal decision. There are a million reasons why someone might come out, and a million reasons why someone might not, but I would like to offer you a different way to look at it. The idea of "**coming out**" only exists because we adults often assume everyone is heterosexual. That is a result of **heteronormativity**, which is when people unfairly and incorrectly think everyone is or should be heterosexual or straight. If we didn't start off assuming everyone was straight, people wouldn't have a need to "come out" at all. Everyone would just be whatever sexuality or gender was true for them and share that information if and when they wanted to.

Being gay, bisexual, trans, or lesbian does not have to feel like a big secret you are hiding from the world. Your sexual identity and your gender are unique parts of what make you, you. Sharing those parts of yourself is a personal choice based on who you desire to know those parts of you. So perhaps it is not about "coming out" at all, but instead about figuring out who you'd like to invite to get to know more of your authentic self.

No matter what you call it, sharing your gender or sexual identity with others is not a one-size-fits-all situation. You may feel comfortable sharing about it in some situations or with certain people and not in other situations or with other people. Some of the questions you might weigh when you're figuring out when or with whom to share could include:

- **Will I be physically safe? (Keeping yourself safe is always a primary concern.)**
- **Will I be treated well emotionally? (Emotional safety is just as important as physical safety!)**
- **How well do I know this person?**
- **Am I usually respected and cared for by this person?**
- **How does this person treat other LGBTQQIA2S+ people in their life or in the media?**
- **Will coming out make me feel relieved and less burdened once I get it off my chest?**
- **Is it important for me that this person knows the realest, most authentic version of me?**
- **Is this someone I want to talk to about my crushes and/or future relationships and eventually introduce people I'm dating to this person?**
- **Is not coming out making me feel bad about myself or like there's something wrong with me?**

Thinking through this list may help you decide when or if there is a right time to invite someone into that part of your identity.

If you choose to share or "come out," I suggest starting with someone who is loving, kind, and supportive. Think about the people who have helped you the most and been there for you in challenging times. Think about the people who make you feel safe and loved in the world. Those are the people who have earned the right to know you on a deeper level. Those are the people I'd come out to.

If you feel like you can't identify anyone who fits that role in your life, there are lots of really good resources for LGBTQQIA2S+ youth online. Here are some websites that have resources, hotlines, articles, and organizations that can help you navigate this important part of your life:

Within the US:
- **CDC LGBTQQIA2S+ Youth Resources: https://www.cdc.gov /lgbthealth/youth-resources.htm**
- **The Trevor Project: https://www.thetrevorproject.org**
- **GLAAD: https://www.glaad.org**
- **GLSEN: https://www.glsen.org**
- **Website of Kate Bornstein, author, activist, and LGBTQQIA2S+ youth advocate: http://katebornstein.com**

Internationally:
- **IGLYO https://www.iglyo.com/ (The International Lesbian, Gay, Bisexual, Transgender, Queer, and Intersex Youth and Student Organization; funded by the Dutch government; it has 95 members in 40+ countries)**
- **LGBT Youth Line: https://www.youthline.ca/ (toll-free hotline in Ontario, Canada)**
- **Ahwaa https://majal.org/ahwaa, an online discussion platform for Arab LGBTQQIA2S+ folks**

- LGBT Youth Scotland: https://www.lgbtyouth.org.uk/
- RainbowYOUTH: https://ry.org.nz/about-us (in Aotearoa NZ)
- Minus18: https://www.minus18.org.au/ (in Australia)
- Pride House Tokyo: https://pridehouse.jp/en (in Japan)
- African Queer Youth Initiative: https://aqyi.org/ (has members located across the continent)
- Le Refuge: https://le-refuge.org/ (LGBT+ youth shelter based in Montpellier, France)

> **QUESTION:** I am aroace (aromantic/asexual) and I don't really know why it's so hard to come out to my parents.

Our adult world so often assumes people will grow up to be **allosexual** (experience sexual attraction for others) and develop romantic relationships as one-half of a couple (also known as **amatonormativity**). They also assume those relationships will be **monogamous**, where two people only have romantic or sexual relationships with each other. Every fairy tale we're told as kids assumes we will eventually fall in love and get married, usually also assuming we'll be heterosexual!

It can feel extra scary to tell our parents that some of those things aren't things we're interested in doing. We might be worried our parents will think there's something "wrong" with us, that we won't fulfill their hopes and dreams for us, or that they'll think we don't really know how we feel because of still being a kid. But they're YOUR feelings, and you know how you feel! You deserve to be respected for your radical honesty and authenticity in sharing your true self with your family. And it's important for your family to consider the fact that asexual-spectrum people still lead full, vibrant lives.

As I discuss above, telling parents and caregivers about our sexual orientations, aka "coming out," may not always be safe depending on your relationship with your caregivers. In cases where there may not be a healthy or loving family dynamic, there can be a risk in letting them know you identify outside of heterosexuality. If you feel like this applies to you, you can seek out resources to connect to others, such as the Asexual Visibility and Education Network (AVEN): https://www.asexuality.org.

Whether you share your aroace identity with them or not, the most important thing is to know and love yourself no matter how you identify and no matter whom you share that with.

> **QUESTION:** Do you believe that sexuality should be assumed, or that parents should say nothing until their child displays a preference?

Making assumptions almost never turns out well. It doesn't matter what we are assuming. We can assume our friend is going to meet us for lunch and wonder why we are all alone at the lunch table. Or we could assume that our teacher knows we had a stomachache and that's why we didn't turn in our homework and then end up with a giant zero on that assignment. Assuming means we don't have the necessary information to make the right call. Similarly, I think making assumptions about anyone's sexuality or gender is likely not to be accurate if they haven't told you.

When parents make assumptions about their kids' sexuality, they tend to assume they're heterosexual. This, again, is part of heteronormativity. Not only does heteronormativity make life harder and more exhausting for LGBTQQIA2S+ people, who have to constantly correct people's assumptions about their lives or worry whether it's even safe to do so, it also leads to **heterosexism**, or the prejudice against—and mistreatment of—people who are not heterosexual. And if our parents are constantly assuming we're heterosexual or are going to be heterosexual when we grow up, it may make us wonder if there's something wrong with us for not feeling that way. It may also make us question whether our parents would be accepting if we let them know their assumptions are wrong.

There are lots of things we may not fully understand about ourselves until we get older, sexuality included. And we should all have the space to explore our identities at each phase of our lives. Our parents' and caregivers' role is to help us do that safely and with love. I think it's important for parents to talk openly about lots of things regarding sexuality, including all the different ways you and other people might experience your sexuality, and to leave room for you to have open, honest conversations about who you are and who you want to be.

GENDER

Ideas about what it means to be male and female, masculine and feminine, boy and girl, woman and man, are what people usually mean when they talk about gender. But what, for example, makes a toy "boyish" or "girly"? What about people who don't fit into the boxes of "boy" or "girl" at all? Gender is a huge, complex idea that doesn't just mean one thing, and there are many ways to have a gender.

For example, people are typically classified as "male" at birth if they have a penis and "female" at birth if they have a vagina. People who continue to identify with the gender they were classified as at birth are considered cisgender. And folks who identify with a gender different from the one they were classified with at birth are considered transgender. People who don't identify strictly as male or female are considered non-binary. There are also people who don't identify with any gender, which is called being **agender**.

Just because we have certain body parts doesn't mean that we should be forced to act a certain way or deny how we most feel comfortable expressing ourselves in the world. As we'll see, gender has changed—and will likely continue to change—across time and cultures, shifting as our societies shift. When you hear someone using the terms "male" and "female," or boy and girl, or man and woman, I want you to keep in mind that there are many ways to be male and female, and that those aren't the only two options either!

Many of you had questions about sexism (discrimination against women and girls), and why people believe various things about gender, or questions about exploring your own genders. We'll get into all of that and more. What you need to know before we begin is that no one should ever be treated unequally based on their gender, and everyone should be able to live their best lives in safety and dignity. If someone tries to tell you otherwise, they're mistaken or trying to be mean—sometimes both. Over here, we value radical love and kindness.

Content note: *In this chapter we will talk about violence against women.*

UNAPOLOGETICALLY ME

QUESTION: It's been a while now, and I've never known who to reach out to about my gender problem. I've been having a love-hate relationship with myself and it's starting to get pretty annoying. At times, I feel comfortable with my birth name and gender but some days I hate it so much and wish I could just be someone new. Is there any way to help with this? I've been debating if I might be non-binary or genderfluid, but this is new to me, so I'm kinda helpless.

The first thing I want you to give yourself is a big old heaping scoop of radical compassion. It really is okay not to have the answers and to be struggling with your gender. There are other people like you who feel different ways about their gender depending on the day. This isn't something to "fix" so much as it is something to explore.

That said, if you've done some exploration and find yourself becoming more and more distressed by it, you do have options. . . .

One of the biggest gifts you can give yourself in your journey is the gift of community, which is radical self-love tool number nine at the end of the book. Building community doesn't just magically happen; it is a skill we have to develop. It requires we look for people who have gone through what we are going through. It is not always easy, but boy is it always worth it. This may mean seeking out non-binary and genderfluid people to see if you have an "aha" moment about your own experiences and identity. If you can't do this in an in-person youth group setting in your local area, you can also look for this community online. You can follow non-binary and genderfluid pages on social media as well as media sources like Them: https://www.them.us. Being in community will remind you you're not alone and can give you ideas about how others have navigated similar issues.

When you say you have a "love-hate" relationship with yourself, that's something we should talk about more. What does it mean to "love-hate" yourself? Is it your possible genderfluid identity that you love and hate sometimes? Or is the love-hate experience coming from deeper feelings of shame and confusion about your identity because of living in a society that doesn't appreciate or embrace gender fluidity?

When we get in touch with our radical self-love, we're able to disrupt feelings of hate toward ourselves and remember that there was never anything shameful about us to begin with. We can do this by practicing tool number five, **Banish the Binary**, which invites us to get rid of either/or thinking or using judgments like good or bad to describe ourselves or our bodies. When you allow yourself to see your gender as an ever-expanding part of your magic, you may be more easily able to honor how it feels different on different days.

Don't let society's limited imagination keep you from seeing the full beauty of your uniqueness. Some of us come to this planet as caterpillars meant to emerge as butterflies, that's all. Or as peacocks strutting all our gorgeous colors. You are never too much to handle in all your gender-expansive glory.

QUESTION: I feel like I am very feminine even though I was born with a male body. I call myself non-binary even though I act feminine. Does this mean I should classify myself as she/her or they/them?

ASK AN EXPERT: Kate Bornstein is a brilliant longtime gender justice activist and artist who has helped so many of my friends understand their gender journey and live full, empowered lives. I was certain Kate could tackle this important question.

Ohhh, that's a very good question and the answer has a few parts to it.

So, you call yourself non-binary. How about that, so do I!

And you act feminine? Me too!

As to pronouns, I've used them all. First, I used he/him. Then I used she/her. For a while, I used ze/hir but no one knew what I was talking about, so I switched to they/them about a year ago. And now? Now I use all of them, and it makes my life so much easier.

Being non-binary, sometimes I come across as a girl, sometimes I come across as a boy, sometimes as both or neither. Very clever people can see that I am both and neither at the same time. But no matter how I come across to people, no matter what they think I might be when they look at me, no matter what pronoun pops into their minds or out of their mouths, I'm still non-binary me and nothing they say can change that, and the same goes for you.

Keeping that in mind, let's get down to the question of you classifying yourself with the pronouns she/her or they/them. Well, that depends on why you'd like to classify yourself with a pronoun in the first place. Is it because you'd like to explain yourself to other people? Maybe it helps you explain yourself to yourself. Both of those are good reasons for classifying yourself with a pronoun. Personally, I like they/them because I'm non-binary and that says non-binary best. But if people do use she/her or refer to me as a girl or a woman? Well, that makes me smile because I enjoy femininity.

But hold on. Maybe you feel you have to classify yourself with a pronoun because everyone else is asking you to do that. If that's the case, then I suggest you tell them to use any pronoun they want. The pronoun they choose will tell you a lot more about them than it could ever say about you.

QUESTION: I am non-binary and like people to use they/them pronouns, but some people laugh at me when I tell them. Why do people make fun of my gender?

Well, aren't those people immature? I offer a big thumbs-down to them.

Unfortunately, we live in a world where society has said that there are only certain ways we get to exist in our bodies and those rules have been particularly strict around gender. For far too long society has said the "right ways" to be in a body include being in a body that is either a boy or a girl, and that this is decided by our genitals.

This outdated idea is called the gender binary. Our ideas about gender often make it difficult for people who experience their gender in ways that are different than simply male or female to feel accepted and supported in our world. People often repeat what it is that they were taught, no matter if those messages are harmful or unjust. You have every right to define yourself.

The gender binary limits all humans' ability—including those whose genders fall inside the binary—to be exactly who we are without society deciding who we should be. That's because trying to fit into the cramped box of the binary takes a lot of work. Men feel the need to be "manly" enough, while women face pressure to be the appropriate amount feminine (but not too feminine, because most societies still equate femininity with weakness and other sexist ideas). Whew, child, the gender binary is just plain exhausting!

Oftentimes, people engage in binary thinking because it feels simpler to just place others in easy-to-understand boxes with familiar labels. I wonder, what would be possible if every human decided it was totally okay for us to NOT be easy to understand (especially since none of us really are)?

Your gender is part of your unique and very personal expression, and there may be people who just don't get it. I promise you don't need them to understand for you to be powerfully you.

One of the coolest things about being powerfully you is that it often gives others permission to do the same. Pretty soon, many of the folks who wanted to make fun of your gender may come to better understand their own genders because you were so committed to being unapologetically you. I have some amazing non-binary activist friends like Alok Vaid-Menon, who wrote the book *Beyond the Gender Binary*, and whose choice to be brave, bold, and unapologetic is helping people every day to expand their ideas about gender.

In the meantime, hold your boundaries. Keep asking for what you need regarding your pronouns. There will be times in all our lives when we must keep demanding respect for ourselves even if people resist giving it.

QUESTION: I'm transgender and I don't know how to decide if I should remove my privates or not.

What you are describing sounds like a type of gender affirmation surgery. Doctors perform this surgery to help trans people, usually adults, align their bodies with how they experience their gender. Gender affirmation surgery is just one aspect of a series of medical options called **gender affirmation treatments** that trans people may undergo. These are big decisions, and you absolutely have time to figure out what feels best for you.

People often consider gender-related medical treatment when they are experiencing **dysphoria**. Gender dysphoria can refer to feeling uncomfortable with your body because it doesn't feel like it "matches" your gender (for example, a trans man no longer wanting to have breasts on his body), and it can also include social dysphoria, where someone feels uncomfortable after interacting with someone who doesn't recognize or disrespects their gender (for example, being misgendered). Someone with social dysphoria doesn't necessarily also experience body-based dysphoria, because like any group of people, not all trans people feel the same way! Keep in mind that genital-related surgery isn't the only way trans people medically transition. For transgender youth, one gender-affirming therapy that could be possible and is far more common for minors is the use of hormone blockers, also called puberty blockers. Hormone blockers suspend the production of estrogen and testosterone, the hormones responsible for puberty changes, including the growth of facial hair, the development of breasts, deepening of voice, periods, and widening hips. The blockers are temporary and are used to stop your body from going through the changes above while you figure out what you want to happen and what is most affirming for your gender.

Some trans people also don't feel the need to transition medically. Some ways that trans people transition non-medically include updating pronouns, choosing a new name, and/or wearing gender-affirming clothing and hairstyles. There is no one right way to be trans, just like there is no one right way to be any type of human! If you are trans, then however you are trans, you are perfectly you. Perhaps this is a time to try out different non-surgical ways of exploring your gender while you sort out the medical questions. Try different clothes and other style choices that feel affirming. Play around and enjoy discovering your own unique gender expression. Explore how you can find happiness in your gender today. When you're able to feel joy in expressing your authentic gender, that is called **gender euphoria**, which is the opposite of dysphoria and is what everyone who has a gender deserves!

Before making any decisions, talking to other trans kids and adults about this will be important, whether online or—if you're able to access any opportunities to do so—offline. Being in community with others who have a similar experience is always a good place to begin finding answers. There are also some gender affirmation surgeons who are trans and offer helpful resources, like Marci Bowers, who is the first known trans woman to have ever performed gender affirmation surgeries. Her website is: https://marcibowers.com.

Remember, there's no right or wrong answer and, most importantly, your transness doesn't depend on whether you've had any specific medical procedure. Practicing radical self-love tool number three, **Reframe Your Framework**, may help make the choice that is best for you. If you see your body as your teammate in achieving your best life, then you and your body can work together and you can do what feels most honest for you.

SILLY GENDER IDEAS

> **QUESTION:** Why is it that if I, as a girl, have a friend who is a boy, people automatically call him my "boyfriend"?

The easiest answer to this question is because people are silly. In this case, the silliness is due to heterosexism, as I mentioned in the chapter on sexuality. But let's back up: We know there are numerous ways people can identify sexually. When men are attracted to and partner with women and women are attracted to and partner with men, that is heterosexuality. Unfortunately, society often values heterosexual relationships over other types of relationships like friendship, whether the people are the same or different genders. When it's assumed that any relationship between a man and woman is sexual in nature, this is an example of heterosexism in action. The next time someone asks you this, you should ask them if their friend who is a dog is a dogfriend.

> **QUESTION:** Are girls really not as good at math and science as boys? I don't think that's true, but I don't get why some people think so.

You are completely correct: Girls are just as capable of understanding any kind of knowledge as boys are. Unfortunately, because of **sexism** (prejudice or discrimination based on the belief that the male sex is superior), whole generations of people grew up being told that math and science are "for" boys, which made them treat girls differently and made it harder for girls to succeed in STEM (science, technology, engineering, and math) careers. Many women continue to face discrimination when trying to pursue STEM careers, which perpetuates and contributes to those fields being filled with men. There is a long history of girls and women having to fight to get the right to an education and disproving the idea that their only role in life is to be wives and mothers. While being wives and mothers is great, women, like men, deserve to have lots of different roles like . . . like, hmmmm . . . president!

There are incredible examples of girls and women challenging these old sexist ideas, even risking their lives to do so. In Pakistan, a young girl named Malala Yousafzai passionately believed in girls' right to go to school and was an outspoken advocate of girls' education. Taliban terrorists, who believed in banning girls from going to school where she lived, then issued a death threat against her and shot her in 2012 when she was only fifteen years old. Malala survived being shot and became a global activist for girls' education, becoming the youngest person to receive a Nobel Peace Prize! She's a reminder that girls can do anything they put their minds to.

QUESTION: Why is pink associated with girls and blue with boys? Was it always this way?

While I ADORE pink (and look great in it, if I do say so myself), no, it was definitely not always this way! According to historian Jo B. Paoletti, children of all genders were dressed in white dresses for centuries in various Western countries until they were six or seven. This didn't change until the mid-1800s, when it became popular to dress babies in pastels, but not in a rigid pink-or-blue gendered way. According to one article from 1918, pink was for boys because it was a "stronger" color, while blue was for girls because it was "dainty"! This is the complete opposite of how the colors are thought of today in most Western societies, where pink is considered "feminine" and blue is considered "masculine." It wasn't until the 1940s that US society shifted toward thinking of pink as a girls' color and blue as a boys' color. Meanwhile in modern India, men as well as women routinely wear pink.

This shows us how gender shifts across time and place. Even though we're taught by our societies that gender simply "is" a certain way, how we understand people's genders is always influenced by our cultures, what time period we live in, and so on. Gender has changed meaning across the centuries and the globe, and will continue to do so!

QUESTION: What is mansplaining?

Let's break it down by parts: the first part being "man," and the second part "-splaining." This is a term used to describe when men explain things to women and others by assuming the person doesn't already know. Mansplaining hurts because often in our society we tell men that they are the authorities on all things. And we often give men very little space to be uncertain or to simply say "I don't know," without feeling like they are failures or not good enough. We also teach women and trans and non-binary people that they are not as smart as men. If you look at old movies where women are portrayed as weak, irrational, emotional, and helpless compared to men, you'll see what I mean.

We see this in fairy tales all the time too—the helpless princess waiting to be rescued by the heroic knight or prince, not knowing how to save herself. That's why more modern kids' movies like *Tangled*, *Encanto*, and *Raya and the Last Dragon* are so important (spoiler alert: They are not about being saved by a prince!).

The result of these sexist messages in society is that some men move through the world assuming that others know less than them or that they have the answer for everything, whether they're certain or not. A good way to work toward getting rid of mansplaining in the world is for boys and men to think before speaking. Question the belief that men are smarter. Listen to and follow women and non-binary people and learn from them. And if you find yourself in a conversation, consider if (and why!) you're assuming that a girl or woman doesn't already know something, and give her equal space to talk and share.

If you experience mansplaining, there are a few strategies you can try. If a boy or man is trying to tell you something you already know, it is okay to speak up and say, "Thanks, but I know about this," and then go on and share the information you have. You can try humorously reminding the person that you have ideas you would like to share too. Lastly, you can explain that they are mansplaining and then share what you learned in this book with them. No matter how you choose to handle it, don't be afraid to share your brilliance.

> **QUESTION:** Why is there so much violence against women in the world?

I wish there was an easy answer to this question. Unfortunately, there is not.

However, there are some root causes that contribute to violence against women around the world. Many societies in our world are governed by a system called **patriarchy** where men hold most of the power and women and other groups are significantly excluded from it. Patriarchy teaches everyone that women are weaker, less intelligent, and should be subservient to or beneath men.

These ideas and the system of patriarchy certainly play a role in the violence. Globally, almost one in three women experience physical and/or sexual violence in their lifetime, according to the World Health Organization. Violence against women takes many forms: intimate partner violence, sexual assault and rape, and the murder of women and girls based on their gender, which is called **femicide**. Most (but not all) of this violence is committed by men against women.

Part of why this happens is because of the harmful messages we teach men about women, but also about themselves. Societies often teach men from an early age that strength and violence are what make a man and that emotions are feminine and wrong. Messages like this are dangerous. Boys are often not taught effective non-aggressive, non-violent ways to handle their emotions or to explore their emotions beyond anger. This creates adult men who may use their physical strength against women in abusive ways or act out in displays of "power over" to intimidate and control. Men must learn better tools of emotional intelligence. Violence against women is NEVER okay.

Feminists (activists for women's and girls' rights and gender equality) have long been fighting all over the world to end violence against women. It was feminist **activism** in the 1970s that led to the creation of women's shelters for women and their kids to stay in when fleeing abuse at home, as well as rape crisis centers, which are organizations that help survivors of sexual violence find healing and safety. There are also resources for men who have committed violence against women to seek help with regulating their emotions and begin healing their abusiveness. Check out www.futureswithoutviolence.org for more information. Books like *Boys Will Be Human* by Justin Baldoni can help boys learn how to manage their emotions in a healthy way.

We all must learn how to be able to experience conflict with each other in healthy, non-violent ways. This includes learning how to have open communication, stepping away from an argument when we're too upset to be kind, and seeking help from professionals like therapists for our negative emotions—remember regulating our emotions?—instead of taking them out on others. We'll have to work together as one planet to help end structures like patriarchy, which hurt all humans and keep us from fully embracing radical love.

Wherever there is a group of people being treated unequally, there are members of that group who will seek freedom—that is a truth among human beings since the beginning of time. So yes, women and girls have been fighting throughout history to be treated equally to men, and in different ways according to their specific situation in different countries, cultures, and historical time periods.

There are countless books and films about such women and girls, from medieval women like Christine de Pizan to the powerful anti-slavery abolitionist Sojourner Truth to the radical activism of British suffragettes—see what you can find at your local library this weekend! Don't forget to learn about the powerful women around the world still fighting, including some of these names and movements: Tarana Burke, Zulaikha Patel, Cori Bush, Lorelei Williams, Line Niedeggen, Elle van der Burg, the Sanandaj anti-veil resistance in Iran, the Glitter Revolution in Mexico, and the Women's March rallies in the US.

You are late, my friend. It's okay, you are not alone; I am always late! There has been a woman as president. There have been quite a few, but it depends on what you mean by president.

Female rulers and leaders (with similar roles to a president) have always existed. Women have governed kingdoms, tribes, monarchies, and nations throughout history. But much of that history doesn't get told because of things like **colonization**, a system in which a nation takes over control and exerts rulership over another nation and erases much of their history and culture.

However, I assure you women have ruled, both well and not so well, throughout time. There was Awashonks of the Wampanoag, for example, who became chief (or sachem) of her people in the 1600s. Her signature is on the Plymouth agreement of 1671. Hatshepsut ascended to the Egyptian throne in around 1479 BCE, casting aside women's clothing and rocking a beard. And Boudica of the Iceni tribe led an army to fight against the Roman occupation of England in 60 or 61 CE.

If you are talking about our more modern definition of president, then the first female appointed head of a country was Sirimavo Bandaranaike, who was appointed prime minister of Sri Lanka in 1960. And the first democratically elected female president was Vigdís Finnbogadóttir, who became the president of Iceland in 1980. Since then, many countries have elected women as leaders. In New

Zealand, Jacinda Ardern became the second woman to have a baby while head of the government. The United States has yet to elect a female president, and there are many factors that have contributed to that, including the serious sexism female politicians face when they run for political office. The US has had its first female vice president, Kamala Harris.

It is important to remember that being a woman does not automatically make a person a good leader or guarantee her policies will be equitable in action, just in principle, or make everyone's lives better. Women, like all humans, also hold oppressive ideas and can treat people in oppressive ways. I, for one, want a president who will truly help create justice for all. Maybe that person will be trans, disabled, or even **undocumented**. Nevertheless, women have shown all over the world that they are just as capable of every kind of leadership as men are and should have all the same opportunities.

RACE AND RACISM

Of all the complicated topics we struggle to talk about in our world, race is one of the biggest. Race shapes how we understand ourselves and how we are experienced by others. It is used to explain the color of our skin and can be associated with our **ethnicity** or where we come from.

The idea of race has played a major part in wars, financial systems, our schools, and society, all while being completely made up. Yes, I said it: *made up*. Race is an idea that was created by humans but has no scientific basis. We are all one race, the human race. Unfortunately, the outcome of race—racism—has shaped all our lives whether we are aware of it or not.

Some people may believe that it's not okay or polite to talk about race; that if we ignore it, we'll all live in harmony. But what happened the last time you ignored the test you had coming up in history class? Yeah, that didn't go well either, did it? The point is, nothing is solved through ignoring or avoiding it. It's important to talk openly about everything, race included! We can't fight injustice and forms of oppression until we understand what they are, how they impact us, and what we can do together to solve them.

Content note: *This chapter involves honestly discussing the history of racist violence against people of color, with an emphasis on genocide and enslavement.*

WHAT'S UP WITH RACISM?

> **QUESTION:** Why are people of all sorts racist?

My oh my, you asked a giant question that you might not realize is giant. But let's try to tackle it. In order to answer your question, it's important to define what racism is and sort it out from other concepts like prejudice and discrimination. **Prejudice** is when we assume negative things about people without really knowing them. You can see its meaning inside the word itself: "pre-" plus "judge." Anyone can have prejudice, which typically comes from unfairly judging someone based on negative stereotypes and myths about a group they're a part of. Discrimination is when we take our prejudiced beliefs and put them into action, treating a person and/or group unfairly as a result.

Racism is the combination of racial prejudice plus power, which results in racial discrimination. What kind of power? Well, the kind of power that lets you use your prejudice toward someone to discriminate against them through major institutions in society, such as the legal system, at school, and in the workplace. It's the power that goes along with your group being given better treatment in society.

Here's an example: Let's say you don't like people who wear purple. Maybe your parents told you that people who wear purple are mean and steal or you just think it is an ugly color. Your ideas make you prejudiced against people wearing purple. Now, if someone wearing purple asked to sit at your table during school lunch and you refused to welcome them, you would be discriminating against a person who is wearing purple because now you have added actions to your prejudiced ideas. Of course, this isn't a kind way to act toward someone just because they like wearing purple clothes, and yes, your actions may hurt their feelings, but you still don't have the power to impact their life in a major way. They can just sit at another table with other people and still have lunch.

Now, let's say you are the lunch monitor and decide who can enter the lunchroom, and you tell all the lunch captains who guard each table, "No purple wearers allowed!" Or let's say you're the school principal, and you decide that purple wearers can't even come to your school. Now your prejudiced ideas and actions have the ability to not only impact one person, but to keep a whole group of people who wear purple from sitting anywhere, having lunch at all, or even going to school. You have the power to restrict a major part of their lives. This is how racism operates.

Racism isn't just about one person not liking another person and being mean to them—it's much bigger than that. It's about one group historically having power over other groups and using that power to oppress them by restricting access to things like housing, jobs, schools, government, and even cultural aspects of their lives, all based on race. In our Western society, white people have historically held much of the power while people of color—Black, Indigenous, Latine, Middle Eastern, and Asian and Pacific Islander people—have been treated unfairly.

Based on our definition of racism as prejudice + power, white people as a group in most Western countries have had social, economic, and political power that people of color as a group have not had. Mix that power with racial prejudice and you get racism. Given that people of color in the US and other Western countries don't have the same social, economic, and political power to oppress white people collectively, we could say people of color can engage in prejudice and discrimination but not necessarily racism.

Now, can people of all sorts be prejudiced? Unfortunately, yes. Humans make all sorts of judgments and stereotypes about others, and all of it is harmful to creating a loving and kind world. However, it is important that we understand that racism and other forms of oppression are not about just being mean. Racism can occur even when someone is not trying to be mean.

Centuries ago, white settlers from European nations moved to the US, Canada, Australia, New Zealand, many countries in Africa and various islands around the world, and claimed them as their own. They built housing, schools, economic systems, and laws based on their ideas and ways of life, despite the Indigenous cultures that already lived there. European colonizers murdered many Indigenous tribes in order to maintain and expand their power. This act is called **genocide**. In so doing, these European colonizers set up harmful infrastructures that have proved to be unsustainable, hurting the land and water and, ultimately, all of us, especially emotionally and spiritually.

In the 1600s, many of those same European nations began stealing people from African countries and forcing them to work for free in these new colonies. The system of slavery lasted for hundreds of years. Acts of genocide were baked into every part of these colonized nations. These actions were clearly wrong, but Europeans told themselves it was okay by claiming to be superior to everyone else based on their skin color. Through violence, they enforced that myth all over the world. This false belief that whiteness is best and deserves greater power is what I refer to as **white supremacist delusion**.

All the systems in the United States have been influenced by white supremacist delusion. Things like the economy, housing, schools, government, laws, and health care have all been impacted. Many of the American systems that were created or expanded under the conditions of slavery and genocide still exist. Those systems were designed to protect the power of white people. Participating in these systems without challenging them or even looking at how they are unequal is racism.

Because people of color are the targets of racism, they have collective but varied experiences with how racism harms them. White people, in contrast, benefit from racism because of the long, complex history I mentioned above. Racism isn't about being bad or mean. It is about the harm that happens from not knowing one's history. In some ways, our society is set up to hide racist parts of history so that white people never have to think about it. That way, racism (prejudice + power) can just keep happening without interruption.

Abolishing racism requires that we understand how race, racism, and white supremacist delusion operate around us. Once we understand how these systems are racist, we can figure out how to replace that racism with radical love and create a society where everyone is cared for and respected.

QUESTION: Why are white people racist
toward Black people?

As a Black person, I wish I could share this question and this answer with everyone in the world so we could end racism toward Black people. But trying to answer your question is a great place to start.

To understand our modern society, we usually need to go back and look at the past to see how we got here. There has been a long history of anti-Blackness (racism toward Black people), and prejudice against people with darker skin for centuries. Many of these anti-Black ideas were spread by Europeans through acts of **colonization** and used as a reason to justify their creation of the transatlantic slave trade. Anti-Blackness, greed, and discrimination are what happen in society when we aren't in touch with our inherent value and enoughness—our radical self-love. This greed and disconnection allowed Europeans to continue the transatlantic slave trade for centuries. This system involved kidnapping and enslaving people from the continent of Africa for labor and profit, colonizing large swaths of the globe, building empires on that enslavement and colonization, and then maintaining anti-Black practices through racist legal, social, and economic structures, such as **Jim Crow** segregation laws in the post–Civil War United States and **apartheid** in South Africa.

Countries like Spain and Portugal were looking for free ways to make more money and sell more goods. To justify stealing humans, they needed to tell themselves that the people they were stealing were beneath them. Early Europeans created and spread the lie that they were a better category of human and that those they terrorized were less human or not human at all.

This is when the concept of **whiteness** came into being. Different groups of Europeans, who had previously fought amongst each other and argued over religion, land, and power, could now unite as white and declare they were superior to others who looked different. And so, white supremacist delusion was born.

It's this history that paved the way for present-day anti-Black racism. As a result of colonization, slavery, and centuries of racist social ideas, many white people today are still taught the lie by their families and white-dominated societies that Black people and anyone with darker skin are less than them. These ideas are reinforced by additional messages saying racism isn't a big deal anymore; that it doesn't exist if no one talks about race. Society is encouraging us to forget history. The United States and most Western societies have been shaped by racist beliefs and behaviors toward Black people, and those ideas are still supported by schools, media, and politics today.

In reality, most white people haven't truly grappled with the history of anti-Blackness in their societies and within their own families, all of which has led to continued discriminatory attitudes and policies toward Black people. The only way to rid our world of anti-Black racism is to collectively acknowledge its current role in society, be honest about our history, and make lifelong efforts to repair it through justice-based policies. White people must actively work to dismantle the beliefs and ideas they may not even realize they have about Black people—understanding that all folks in Western countries internalize anti-Black racism in one way or another because it's become part of the very air we breathe.

And nobody is better positioned to change the history of racism than young people, who know the truth and can take action toward change.

WRESTLING WITH PRIVILEGE

> **QUESTION:** What is white privilege?

White privilege is the bundle of unearned advantages white people have access to just by being born white in a racist society. Researcher Peggy McIntosh has famously called it an "invisible knapsack" (or backpack) because of how this privilege equips white people with a bunch of tools that help them be treated better in society compared to people of color—but it's invisible because white people don't usually know it's there or that they're carrying it around with them. It includes both the ways white people are treated better than people of color as well as the things white people never have to deal with or be aware of because they're not the ones experiencing racism.

For example, from 1993 to 2013 the New York City Police Department used a policy called "Stop and Frisk" to stop, question, and potentially arrest anyone they found suspicious. Through racial profiling, the policy overwhelmingly stopped and harassed Black and Latine people, no matter if they had done anything wrong or not. Black and Latine communities felt unsafe and under attack due to this policy. Given that white people were not targeted in the policy, they were less likely to feel its negative impacts.

It's important to point out that white privilege doesn't mean white people never have a hard time or experience real challenges.

All humans have hard times and struggles. Nor does white privilege stop a white person from experiencing different types of oppression, such as sexism, **classism** (being treated badly due to not being wealthy), ableism, transphobia, or homophobia. But whatever their life experiences, privilege ensures the challenges white people have will not be because of their racial identity.

QUESTION: I am a young white girl and I want to be a good ally. I know what kinds of conversations I ought to have with my white friends and family. Do you have suggestions as to how to have those conversations?

ASK AN EXPERT: As I have mentioned, I am not white! But I know some awesome white people navigating the work of being a good ally. I reached out to my fabulous friend and coworker Dr. Shannon Weber to answer this question. She is the author of three books on social justice and is also the Director of Digital Learning at The Body Is Not an Apology. Here are her thoughts.

This is such an important question, and it's one that all young white people should be working together to solve. If white people came together as a group to seriously address the reality of white supremacist delusion, took accountability for the historical and ongoing harm done to people of color, and implemented the ideas for justice and healing that people of color have been fighting for and writing about for centuries, the system of racism could be effectively dismantled.

Know that your attempts at righting these wrongs in your own life are part of that larger project of **right relationship**. I think of right relationship as how we treat each other when we are connected to our radical self-love. We honor each person's dignity and see them as valuable and worthy just for existing. Right relationship encourages us to do our part to fix the systems and circumstances that were built before we as humans understood our radical self-love. This means we would all be working toward love, justice, and compassion for all beings on the planet.

When talking to your fellow white friends and family members, speak from your heart and explain why ending racism is important to you. Focus on the actions of white people—what you've learned and observed about white folks' racism and your desire for white people to contribute differently to the world. Explain what kind of person you want to be in the world and how that vision is different from white supremacist delusion.

Once you start having these discussions, over time you'll be able to become strategic and see which approaches work the best with different people. Your mom might be interested when you tell her about a new documentary you watched about racism, and you can encourage her to watch it and share your thoughts with each other on what you both learned. Your uncle may be less open to seeking out his own education, but you might impact others in a positive way when you refuse to laugh at his racist jokes during the holiday dinner and instead ask him what he finds funny about them. And your friends will come to know what behavior you won't stand for and how you can be depended upon to uphold anti-racist values. These interventions won't always be pleasant—in fact, they can rapidly go from awkward to downright uncomfortable at times. But when was being comfortable or staying silent an effective way for white people to fight racism? (Spoiler: Never!)

You may find that different friends and family members will react differently to what you have to say. Some will be more defensive than others. Some will be angry and try to justify racism or claim they're not racist even though you've witnessed otherwise. And some will welcome open dialogue on the subject. Try to remain patient, within reason—you don't have to tolerate verbal abuse, for example, but also try to remember that everyone's learning has to start somewhere. Check out the "Race" tab of The Body Is Not an Apology's (www.thebodyisnotanapology.com) online Article Library for further resources and ideas as you navigate these thorny but necessary conversations!

QUESTION: If people are being racist to mixed people like myself, doesn't that mean they are actually being racist to themselves? Considering they are usually white themselves and I'm HALF white?

I like the way you think, friend. But first and most importantly, racist ideas do not make much sense. They are ridiculous beliefs that are unfortunately incredibly dangerous.

If you recall, earlier I shared the definition of racism as racial prejudice + power. Historically, one of the ways white people maintained power and control was by deciding who was white. Because whiteness in the United States meant freedom and Blackness meant free labor, it was useful for enslavers and those who supported them to have strict guidelines about who was white and who was not. The US states where slavery was legal decided that any amount of Black blood made a person Black. This policy was called the "**one-drop rule**," and it effectively made anyone with any Black family relations eligible for enslavement. It also allowed white people to claim whiteness as pure. This meant that even mixed-race people were considered Black and, under slavery, considered "less than" white people. Because enslavers often sexually abused enslaved women, the babies that were born from this abuse were still born into slavery, even if they had a free white father.

As we have talked about, these historical policies have shaped our present-day beliefs, and far too many white people still believe that their white skin and white family make them superior to others. It is a sad way to move through the world and a clear example of what happens when we are detached from our radical self-love. When we are in touch with our radical self-love, we don't need to be better than other people because we know we are enough just as we are. It is possible to embrace and love all of your identities, even in a world where people will try to tell you who you are. Radical self-love reminds us that no one knows us better than we know ourselves.

WHO DOES IT HURT?

QUESTION: Why do my cousins, who are Indigenous like me, make jokes about how dark my skin is?

I'm truly sorry that your cousins are making these "jokes" at your expense. They are probably trying to work through understanding how race works in the racist world we live in, but it's still not okay for them to hurt your feelings.

It sounds like you could be experiencing **colorism**, which refers to how lighter skin is valued more than darker skin even among people of color. Colorism is born from anti-Blackness. Colorism subjects darker-skinned people to greater oppression and offers greater privileges to people who look closer to white. It's a tool of white supremacist delusion to turn people of color against each other while maintaining the illusion that whiteness is what everyone should want to look and be like. (You know how we see light-skinned people of color represented more on TV and valued as more "beautiful" by society? That's because of colorism.)

Now that you understand what colorism is, it's easier to see how your cousins' teasing is most likely directly related to their own internalized racism. **Internalized racism** is when those of us who are people of color end up thinking racist thoughts about our worth and value because of what our racist societies teach us from the time we're born. We're not even usually aware that we're thinking or feeling these things because they're lodged so deep down inside of us. We lose touch with our radical self-love through internalized racism and we don't even know it!

This internalized racism leads to colorist comparisons of our skin tones like what you experienced with your cousins. Think about it: There would be nothing "funny" about your darker skin if your cousins didn't internalize deep down that your family, and your larger Indigenous community, should all be as close to white as possible.

When I say that racist and colorist messages start to impact us when we're extremely little, I'm talking not only from personal experience but also from what research tells us. In the 1940s, there was a study done in the US by psychologists Kenneth and Mamie Clark that came to be called the "Doll Tests." In these tests, the Clarks showed Black children, ages three to seven, four different dolls that were the same except for their skin color. They then asked the kids which doll they liked the best. Most kids chose the white doll as the one they liked the most and wanted to play with. They also associated the white doll with positive words but associated the Black dolls with negative words. Some kids even got upset when they were asked which doll looked the most like themselves, since they'd have to pick a Black doll they disliked.

This is a powerful example of why many people of color choose not to think about internalized racism. It can be incredibly painful to become aware of the negative ideas we have been taught about ourselves. Researchers Toni Denese Sturdivant and Iliana Alanis found similar results when they re-created this study in 2020, finding that young Black girls mistreated and stepped on Black dolls in ways they didn't with white dolls. These studies give us powerful examples of how even the smallest kids develop internalized racism.

The good news is that if we work together, we don't have to stay stuck in these horrible systems of colorism and internalized racism. This is where finding our radical self-love and using that love for anti-racist activism come in. When we realize that we have inherent worth, value, and irreplaceable uniqueness, we start to realize that it's racism that's wrong, not us! That's information you can pass on to your cousins and be an example of how we can direct our focus to change society instead of our incredible selves.

> **QUESTION:** As an Asian person, how can I respond to my non-Asian friend telling me that something isn't racist against Asian people because their other Asian friend told them it wasn't?

What a good question! So let me start by saying that not all people in racial or ethnic groups believe the same things. Marginalized groups, just like all groups, contain a diverse range of people with all kinds of opinions and life experiences. This means, as you probably already know, that 100 percent of Asian people won't feel a certain way about a given issue, just like 100 percent of queer people won't think alike or 100 percent of disabled people won't think alike.

I disagree with Black people and other queer people all the time! Just because another Asian person disagreed about something being anti-Asian doesn't mean that they are correct or that evidence of anti-Asian racism is fake, or that you or other Asian people's perspectives are meaningless. It's also important to remember that many people struggle with internalized racism like we mentioned in an earlier question. This may mean that they deny or ignore oppression to avoid difficult feelings or to try and get access to some power in a world rooted in oppression.

Let's dig deeper: The role of a good ally is to listen to the experiences of marginalized groups and work to support them. Like any good friend, they should listen and want to learn more about issues that you are navigating and try to better understand why the situation or idea you shared with them could be considered anti-Asian. A good ally—a good friend—does not try to deny the reality of your experience.

With that, you should ask your non-Asian friend what they are trying to get out of this interaction with you. Are they interested in supporting you or debating your experience? You can also remind them that Asian identity is made up of many different groups and cultures and not all Asians think the same. Just because one person isn't harmed by an idea or situation doesn't mean that idea or situation is harmless to everyone. It's so important that we listen to each other's experiences when we don't have to face a type of discrimination that our friends do. That's called being a good friend.

This is a question that many of us continue to ask every day. You're right, of course, that it shouldn't be shocking or controversial for anyone to want Black people's lives to be protected and cherished. We should want that for every human on the planet! However, our long global history of oppression against Black people is also at the root of why there is so much anger against the movement to protect Black people's lives from racist violence. When we look honestly at our past, we can see why all these anti-Black reactions continue to exist.

Many white people, and even other non-Black people of color, (whether they are actively aware of it or not) have been raised to believe negative stereotypes regarding Black people. Some of those stereotypes include ideas like Black people are lazy, dangerous, more likely to be criminals, and other damaging lies. These myths about Black people began with a long and complex history that goes all the way back to when Europeans started kidnapping African families in Central Africa and the West African coast and brutally enslaving them for profit from the 1500s to the 1800s. Europeans created myths about Black people being dangerous to justify treating them horribly and to distract from the crimes against humanity that Europeans themselves were carrying out against Black and Indigenous people. "Don't look at us! Look over there . . ."

Today, Black folks are often viewed through the same myths of danger that were used so long ago. No matter whether we are walking down the street, playing on a playground, or gathering to protest for justice, we are often treated unfairly or seen as dangerous. These same myths too often lead US police officers to use unnecessary force on Black people, even killing them. As Black people fight for equality and justice, those who believe the myths about us worry that they will lose power, and choose to see the Black Lives Matter movement through the eyes of those old and harmful myths.

You may have heard some people saying the phrase "Black lives matter" is "racist" because "all lives matter!" This is silly and untrue. We know Black people can't be racist against white people because white people are the group with greater power and privilege in society. Remember: Racism is prejudice *plus* having the power to *enforce* your prejudice.

Another reason is that some people believe pointing out racism is being racist. This is called "**reverse racism**" and it is not a real thing. Reverse racism isn't possible, unless we could somehow travel back in time and give the power to people of color and they went on and made the same racist laws against white people that were made against them. Since no one has invented time travel, we know that isn't the reality of racism. Yes, anyone can be prejudiced, but everyone does not have the same power to turn that prejudice into social rules and laws. Everyone doesn't have the power to create racism. When you really think about it, responding to people caring about Black people's lives by saying "But all lives matter!" is just plain weird. Let's say a bully punches your friend at the park and your friend needs help. If you ignored your friend's bloody nose and instead said, "You're not the only one who's hurt! Other people have bloody noses too. All noses matter!" you might find yourself without a friend pretty quickly.

It's as simple as this: When people need our help, we should help them. And if we make excuses not to help, it's probably because we didn't want to help them after all. Not to mention that if you really think all people's lives matter . . . you'd care about Black people's lives and the things that are harming them. You would also care about immigrants' lives. And disabled people's lives. And trans people's lives. And poor people's lives.

And you'd be fighting to end oppression and injustice for all people, because that's what we do when we think people matter.

HOW DO WE FIX IT?

> **QUESTION:** My family told me that it's better to "look past people's color" because we're all just people. Do you think this is a good way to end racism?

Your family probably means well with that advice, but I am going to answer your question with my favorite phrase: Nope. Nope. Nope-ity Nopesville.

"Looking past" people's color is not a good way to end racism. Unless a person is invisible (which would make them a ghost, and this would be a totally different, creepier book), it is not possible to look past someone's color. Their color is part of them, and to ignore it is to ignore important parts of their identity. The not-so-great advice your family is giving you has a name: It's called **color blindness**. And while those who suggest using it may have good intentions, ignoring each other's differences and pretending they don't exist does way more harm than good.

One of the most important steps in practicing radical self-love is learning to make peace with difference. Too many of us have been taught that difference is a bad thing or a problem. When we want to show unity we say, "We are all the same." But the truth is, we are not all the same.

The history of racism has shaped how people have experienced life and what schools they've attended, languages they've spoken, and opportunities they've had. To pretend we are the same is to leave the system of unequal power just like it has always been: unequal. We can't stop racism until we acknowledge how we are different and address how those differences have been used to give some people more power and others less.

This is true no matter if we have white privilege, able-bodied privilege, straight privilege, or any other unfair advantage. If we ignore our differences, how will we see when people of color are being treated unfairly?

While it's true that we are all part of the human family, we don't all have the same experiences, cultures, languages, religions, and so on. And that's an awesome and exciting thing! Imagine if all food tasted the same? YUCK! GROSS! SAD!

Food is better because of difference. Humans are better because of our differences. The work is to learn to see and value everyone's differences. Let's learn about each other and respect what makes us radically us.

QUESTION: How do I start getting involved with activism against racism?

I love, love, *love* when kids ask this question! The world is ready and needs young people just like you to get involved in anti-racist activism every day, starting today!

There are some phenomenal kids out there already doing phenomenal anti-racist activism. For example, when Asean Johnson of Chicago, Illinois, was nine, he became the youngest speaker at the "Realize the Dream" rally that honored the fiftieth anniversary of the March on Washington led by Dr. Martin Luther King, Jr. Asean spoke about how his school and other schools with mostly Black and Latine students in Chicago were having their school budgets cut, with many schools being forced to close. Asean's activism helped stop his school, Marcus Garvey Elementary School, from being closed!

You can attend rallies and protests and marches with your friends or family, and even speak at them like Asean. You can write letters speaking out for racial justice to the editor of your local newspaper or your local politician. You can volunteer at a racial justice organization, get others to join you in creating a petition, or start a fundraiser to support a local family or group. (Everyone likes bake sales, or at least they love cookies! . . . Okay fine, I love cookies.) You can also ask your family to join a **boycott**, which is when people protest corrupt companies by refusing to buy their products and spreading the word until the company agrees to change their behavior.

It's also worthwhile to think about how you will incorporate anti-racism into your life when you grow up. How will you be anti-racist at your future job? If you go on to have kids of your own someday, what would you want to teach them about being anti-racist? What are other ways you can commit to disrupting racism in your daily life? Every action you take matters. Together we can build a world of equity and justice, which is something we all deserve.

FAMILIES

There are so many types of families! For example, families can be made up of you and your parent, two moms or two dads and their children, or siblings being raised by their grandma or aunt or foster parent. Regardless if you have a mom and a dad, whether you're adopted or have a stepdad or live with your older adult siblings—*love* and *connection* are what make a family, not the arrangement of the people inside it, or even how they're related. In my case, I am lucky to have family all over the world, and I am not related to most of them. I call them my chosen family. I have sisters in California and Pennsylvania, aunties in New Zealand, and brothers in Mexico. None of them are related to me by blood, but we are all connected by the love we have for each other and the care we offer each other throughout our lives.

As we explore your questions about being part of your family, we will also talk about the hard parts of family: getting separated from family, family members who aren't safe to be around, and times when we need support from family members but don't receive that support. In short, families are complicated, but they can also be one of our greatest gifts. Let's talk about it!

Content note: *In this chapter we discuss traumatic family experiences, such as poverty, deportation, and substance abuse (abusing drugs and alcohol).*

DIFFERENT SHAPES AND SIZES

QUESTION: I'm adopted, and my birth mom had an open adoption with my adoptive family, which means I was able to know her identity growing up and be in contact with her. While I've met her and had some visits with her, I haven't talked to her very much about why she placed me for adoption. I feel awkward bringing it up and have complicated feelings about it. I also don't want to make my parents feel bad by letting them know I'm struggling. How do I talk about it?

ASK AN EXPERT: Jeanne Greene is a brilliant dancer, a fantastic cook, a mom, and my big sister! She was placed for adoption as a baby and found us, her birth family, as an adult. We even realized we went to high school together without knowing we were sisters. Wild, right? Jeanne has lots of wisdom to share with you on this subject.

Thank you so much for asking this important question. While my adoption was not an open adoption, I have had the privilege and the honor of having my birth family in my life for twenty-five years, and my son has had them in his life since he was born.

I believe this is because I was able to remember as an adoptee that I didn't need to feel like I had to apologize for my existence and how other people felt about the questions I had. I was not responsible for the decisions that resulted in my birth or adoption, and neither were you. But I did deserve answers, and so do you.

When I told my adoptive family that I found my birth family, my adoptive parents didn't say too much. However, when I told them that I wanted to have everybody over my house for a holiday dinner, my mother came and brought my little niece with her. But my father did not come. And I remember asking my [adoptive] father, "Daddy, why aren't you coming? I want you to come. I want you to meet the family . . . my birth family." And he said, "I don't ever need to meet them. You're my daughter."

After hearing his answer, a part of me felt like, "Wow, I really understand how much this man loves me." But the other part of me felt like, "Why don't you want to meet these people? Why don't you want to meet this piece of me?" What I had to remember, and what I encourage you to remind yourself, is that other people's issues are not your responsibility. Your responsibility is to get your own truth and unload your own bags.

You are not responsible for the way in which you came into this world, and you're not responsible for the decisions that other people made regarding you. But you are absolutely responsible for getting your truth and trying to get answers to your "whys." Now, will all your "whys" be answered in the way in which you want them to be answered? No, but you deserve to seek them out. You don't want to spend your life saying, "Oh, I should've asked this," or "I really wish I knew that."

Your adoptive parents may wonder why you want to talk more with your birth mother. They may wonder why you "care about the past." What's most important is to remember that their wondering "why" has nothing to do with you, and everything to do with how they might be feeling about it.

My dad's "why" had nothing to do with me and everything to do with his own feelings. Perhaps he felt anger at my birth parents for letting me go. I don't know, and it wasn't for me to worry about. If I said, "Oh my gosh, he doesn't wanna meet them; well, maybe I just shouldn't have a relationship with them," just imagine what I would have robbed myself of. What I would have robbed my son of.

You're not responsible for the decisions that adults made for you when you just got on this earth. You're also not responsible for their feelings. They will be okay. But you are responsible for making sure that you are okay as you go on this journey, which will be complicated at times.

It's been twenty-five years for me and there is still hurt that comes up. But there are also new joys, new memories that have been created. Trust yourself, because all you are responsible for is making sure that your heart is okay.

QUESTION: I live with my aunt and my cousins. I look up to my aunt so much and how hard she works to take care of me. How come so many TV shows and movies don't have families that look like the one I live in? It's always a mom and dad or maybe a single mom or single dad.

What a smart question! You're right: Way too many television shows, and media in general, focus on the idea of the heterosexual **nuclear family**—a married mom and a dad and their (usually) two kids and maybe a dog.

There are many reasons for this, and most of them relate to concepts we have addressed in this book already. Media companies and the advertising companies who pay them through the sale of commercials are mostly owned and operated by heterosexual white men who likely grew up in families that looked like what is programmed on television. The truth of most media is that it reflects the lives of the people who make it and own it. This becomes a problem when power isn't equal in a society. Tons of people never get to see their reality represented.

When we don't see ourselves, our families, or our lives in the media, we can think it is because we are weird or not worthy of being seen. It can make us think something is wrong with us. I want to remind you loudly, like I am yelling, "THAT IS NOT TRUE!"

The truth is people are in SO MANY different types of families. This includes but is not limited to different generations living together; multiple families living together in one home; families headed by grandparents, aunts, uncles, and older siblings; families with single parents; families with queer and trans parents; and families made up of friends who care about and look after each other. All these different kinds of families are valid and important, and deserve to be seen.

The media we watch should try to show that reality as much as possible, just as it should show the reality that most families aren't wealthy and don't live in huge houses with designer kitchens, and some people are actually allergic to dogs!

Having representative media can help us feel more seen and understood. And we need to make sure all kinds of people from all kinds of families get to make media decisions. Then, I imagine, we will finally see television shows that remind us what makes a family: love, connection, support, and safety, regardless of the arrangement of the people in it.

> **QUESTION:** How do parents of the same gender have children?

There are many ways that parents of the same gender can have kids, just as there are many ways parents of different genders might have kids.

For example, same-gender parents can adopt and be foster parents. Two moms can visit a sperm bank and then one of the moms can implant that sperm inside her body to get pregnant. Two dads can use some of their sperm and seek out a **gestational surrogate**, which is someone who agrees to carry the couple's baby inside their body, gives birth to the baby, and gives the baby to the couple.

These are just some of the possibilities. Many of these ways of having children are also used by heterosexual couples who may have a difficult time getting pregnant or having a baby. Some people will simply choose whatever feels right to them. The most important thing to remember is that, regardless of the process through which parents get to dream of and finally meet and bond with their children (SING IT WITH ME NOW): Love is what makes a family.

FUSSING, FIGHTING, FIGURING IT OUT

QUESTION: Why is it so hard to tell our parents what we actually feel?

There can be many reasons why we find it hard to tell our parents what we're feeling. For one, we're not always sure if we can trust our feelings. And we're not always sure if we can trust our parents' response.

Maybe we feel like they won't understand. Sometimes they won't, but the practice is always about being our most honest and authentic selves, even when people may not understand.

On occasion, we may feel like being honest about our feelings will change how our parents feel about us. But it's important for you to know that healthy relationships have room for honesty, challenges, and dealing with hard stuff—but always with love.

If you know your parents love you because they demonstrate it in how they treat you, then it may be worth taking on the brave challenge of practicing sharing your feelings.

QUESTION: I'm the only girl in a family with three brothers, and my parents treat me differently as a girl. My mom expects me to clean and cook for my brothers while I watch them sit around! It really bothers me. Why does my family do this to me?

Well, none of this sounds fair at all! And unfortunately, you're not alone in experiencing it.

Many of our caregivers were raised with specific ideas about gender—also informed by differences in culture, nation, religion, and more—and ideas about what is "appropriate" for girls versus boys. These ideas are called **gender norms**, and in our society, gender norms are often closely related to sexism and patriarchy.

Often, girls are expected to cook, clean, and take care of the home and boys are expected to run, play, fight, and hold power outside of the home. This organization of society has kept many girls from feeling like they're smart enough or able to do what boys do just as well. And it's kept boys from learning how to communicate and build more caring relationships without being worried about looking tough. Sexism sucks for everyone!

It's weird to imagine, but our parents and caregivers were once kids, likely wondering why they were being treated differently based on their gender too! But instead of realizing that these boring, out-dated rules were ready for the trash can, your folks may have decided that "this is just how it is." And then they passed them on to you like decades-old leftovers. Yuck!

But it is important to recognize that adults are often just sharing ideas they learned as kids. Some of those messages are good and some less good. You will have to learn how to balance where they're coming from, while also listening to yourself and your feelings and speaking up about what you desire.

Have you tried to talk to your family about why they do this and how it makes you feel? They might not even notice they're doing it. They might be willing to hear you out and consider your perspective. It's also possible they could feel defensive or tell you that they believe there should be different roles for boys and girls. How they react to you, and whether you feel safe enough to bring it up to them, will depend on your relationship with your family.

Here's the truth: While there may be different rules for you and your siblings based on age, size, grades, and who knows what else, treating people differently based on gender isn't equitable, and it isn't fair. People of all genders should know how to do various chores because it will help them learn how to be a responsible adult who can wash their own dishes! Your brothers are actually missing out on incredibly important life skills.

The good news in all of this is that you don't have to follow these gendered rules forever. Eventually, you will be an adult, and one of my favorite things about adulthood is how we generally get to decide how to live our lives and what rules make sense for us. While I can't promise the rules in your house will change and your brothers will have to pick up the dish soap and get to scrubbing, I do know there is no limit on what you can do or achieve in the world. Many girls who have felt the way you do have grown up and gone on to do amazing things, including fight for gender equality and other forms of liberation!

Hold on: That could be you too.

First, I am sorry that you feel worried and sick about your family's money issues. It makes total sense that you would want to help your family out of such a stressful situation.

Loving our families makes us want to help and support them. I also imagine that trying to help them might make you feel like you have some power and control over a situation that may feel huge and scary sometimes. Maybe you are thinking that if you could help, your family would stop fighting and you could have a peaceful home life.

Again, all of this makes sense and yet, here's what I want you to know: It's not your job to figure out the money issues in your family. You are not the parent. Sometimes, kids are put in positions where they feel like they have to be the adults—for example, taking care of their younger siblings all the time because a parent is working, addicted to drugs, incarcerated, or dealing with a mental illness. And sometimes, kids are forced to listen to their caregiver's problems and emotional difficulties each day. It sounds like you might be dealing with the latter.

No matter the example, that's a lot of responsibility! Too much!

Scientifically, kids' brains are still developing and don't have all the mental or emotional tools to handle such major issues. It's an unhealthy amount of stress to deal with! There's a term for this that psychologists use called **parentification**—being forced to act as a parent to your caregiver instead of being able to act like their kid. Being pushed into this role in our families can have long-term negative consequences, including developing depression and anxiety as an adult.

Not everyone's parents are able to act like the parents we need them to be. This can be due to their own stress and the difficult things they've gone through in life that they haven't necessarily been able to heal from, known as **trauma**. But while it's not up to kids to figure out their family's financial problems, you *can* take steps to keep your own stress down, and work to feel more secure and safe while your family is fighting. This can include listening to calming music, creating a relaxing space in a corner of your room, finding a physically and emotionally safe space outside where you can recharge (like a favorite tree), and identifying any safe people in your life who you can talk to about your feelings, or safe places you can go to escape the fighting and yelling.

What's most important is remembering that you didn't create the financial troubles in your family, and it is not your job to fix them. But you absolutely can ask for the support and care you need to stay safe and well.

QUESTION: Ever since I can remember, my mom has been on a diet. Even though she doesn't say anything mean or hurtful about my body, she makes negative comments about her own body all the time. It makes me worry my body isn't good enough and that maybe I should be on a diet too. Is this true? What should I do?

Remember how I talked about weight and the global Body Shame Profit Complex in the Bodies section? That is likely what's going on for your mom. She has heard negative messages about her body for such a long time, she has come to believe them. And now it seems she is, like so many people, trying to change her body so it will look the way society has told her it "should" look.

I'm sure that if she could choose, she wouldn't want you to be negatively impacted by these messages too. But even if she doesn't want her own body shame to spread to her child, that's what is happening here. Body shame has a sneaky way of doing that—it spreads among people, especially from adults to kids when kids are trying to look to the adults in their lives for messages about how they should be viewing their own bodies.

Kids should definitely not be on diets. Kids should be playing, laughing, learning, eating, and growing. The more that kids are able to grow up loving their bodies instead of being taught to fear and shrink them, the more we'll have a future where kids and adults alike love their bodies. Remember: If we all loved our bodies just as they are, the diet industry would go bankrupt.

Having a conversation with your mom might be a powerful way for you to share with her how her dieting and negative self-talk are impacting you. It seems like you love her, and my hunch is she loves you too. Sharing that love might be a beautiful start to the both of you beating back the Body Shame Profit Complex together!

QUESTION: My family are immigrants, and my uncle who is undocumented got deported recently. I feel like I can't talk about this with anyone at school. I hear kids tell racist jokes against immigrants and most of my friends can't relate to what I'm going through anyway. I also don't want to get other undocumented family members in trouble by telling someone what I'm going through. How do I deal with how scared and alone I feel?

First, I'm so sorry this has happened to your uncle. And I'm equally sorry to hear that the kids at your school are being racist. Their "jokes" are a form of **xenophobia**, which is the fear and hatred of people considered "foreign." The US has a long and nasty history of xenophobia, even though unless someone is Indigenous and/ or a descendant of enslaved Africans, it is pretty much guaranteed everyone else in the US is an immigrant. You and your family have just as much right to be treated with care and dignity as anyone else, and I hope you never forget that!

It makes sense that you would be feeling scared and alone because of all of this. It might help you to know that, at least statistically, you're not alone: As of 2015, 5.3 million or 10 percent of the US student population was undocumented or lived with a parent who didn't meet the legal requirements to be classified as a US citizen.

Consider talking to other family members about how you're feeling. I'm sure you're not the only one feeling upset, afraid, and isolated. Adults will often try to appear strong to help the kids in the family feel safer, but your uncle's deportation must be hard on everyone. Sharing our feelings can go a long way in helping everyone feel less alone while getting heavy emotions off our chests.

Beyond your family, there are other ways you can find community and connection with other young people who have undocumented family members or who are themselves undocumented. If you have access to the Internet, check out the #UndocumentedAndUnafraid movement, which is fighting back against the fear and stigma targeting undocumented immigrant families through protest and public conversations about what it means to be undocumented. You can also reach out to youth organizers on social media and the local chapters of national organizations for immigrant justice. One great resource is Movimiento Cosecha: https://www.lahuelga.com.

CHOOSING SIDES

QUESTION: My parents are divorced, and my dad tells me when he's mad at my mom and the things he doesn't like about her. Meanwhile my mom is upset a lot and tells me about how upset my dad made her when they were married. It makes me feel like my parents want me to pick sides and choose one of them over the other. Is this normal?

Divorce can be hard on everyone involved, but especially young people. The situation you're describing is, unfortunately, an experience that a lot of kids have with their divorced or unhappily married parents.

But no matter how common the experience, it is not okay for adults to put their stress and unhappiness on a kid. Your parents should be processing their difficult emotions about their marriage and divorce with other adults—specifically therapists—not with you. You are not a therapist, no matter how smart and mature you may be.

You said you feel like they want you to pick "sides." The pressure of hearing your parents talk poorly about each other could certainly add to the feeling of needing to pick a side. But it's important for all of us to learn how to feel our feelings without letting them dictate our actions. I say this because, while your parents may be making you uncomfortable or even hurting your feelings with their comments about each other, you don't have to do anything beyond loving them both. It's your parents' responsibility to realize that their relationship with each other is separate from their relationship with you, and that you should want to have a loving relationship with both your parents (assuming they both treat you with consistent love and care).

The next time one of your parents asks you to side with them, it's completely appropriate for you to ask for a boundary. You can request that they don't say mean or hurtful things about each other in front of you, and then you can say something like, "I'm not going to pick a side. I love you both."

QUESTION: I think that I should tell the truth, but I don't know if I should tell my mom about my dad's girlfriend.

Adults can be messy and complicated. And it's never appropriate for an adult to ask a child to keep a secret. I don't know if that's what your father asked you to do, but you should know that you're not required to keep the secrets of adults. It's an unfair position to put you in, and secrets are often like a toxic fog: They blanket everything and erode trust and connection between people. They are a bad idea, especially with people we love. You are not obligated to keep secrets for adults.

However, I think you might want to consider that you don't know everything about your parents' relationship. Your parents may not have agreed to be monogamous (that is, to only be with each other).

It is possible that your parents have chosen to be in a non-traditional arrangement in which they have other partners, also known as **poly-amory**. The point is, there are things about your parents' relationship structure that you may not know about, nor do you necessarily need to know about, because it is their relationship(s) and their partner-ship, not yours.

Consider talking to a trusted adult and asking for help in navigating the situation and your feelings about it. Some stuff is way too big to try to handle on our own. This sounds like one of those things.

QUESTION: Is it bad if I like living with my foster family more than I like living with my mom? It makes me scared when she drinks and does drugs, but I also don't want her to think I stopped loving her. I feel so confused.

Friend, it is not bad for you to like living in an environment that makes you feel safe and secure. It makes complete sense that you would have some confusing and complex feelings about living with your foster family versus your mom. I know this experience well from my own personal life: I also had a mother who had issues with drink-ing and drugs, and while I loved her very deeply, I also didn't always feel safe being around her. Telling her that I couldn't be around her while she was struggling with drugs and alcohol made me feel like I was betraying her. It took me many years to learn that I was not betraying my mother at all—I was doing what I needed to do to care for myself and keep myself safe. My choice didn't mean I loved her any less. If anything, I loved her so much that I didn't want to watch her keep making choices that caused her to suffer. All I could do was keep reminding her—and myself—of that truth.

I have an idea I talk about often that explains how we deal with issues that seem to have more than one answer or appear to be complicated. I call this the **"great both/and."** While we wish life were as easy as deciding our favorite flavor of ice cream, the truth is that life can be complex, and so are our feelings. At times, we may feel very different emotions all at once, and all those feelings are valid—both/and.

Of course, you can BOTH love your mom deeply AND want to feel safe and protected. You can appreciate BOTH how your foster family takes care of you AND miss your mom. Your mom can BOTH love you AND not be able to provide what you need right now due to how alcohol and other drugs are impacting her body and mind. All of the above can be true for you and are totally acceptable ways to feel—no guilt needed.

I think it would be helpful for your mental health if you could talk about these feelings with someone you trust. This could be a therapist (if you have one!), school counselor, or another adult who consistently treats you with love and respect. From personal experience, I can say that having a therapist helped me so much as I worked through my both/and feelings regarding my mom.

Another way to calm your mind and help you sort through your feelings is to put pen to paper. Start a journal or diary where you write down how you're feeling at the end of each day or week. If you're concerned about privacy, you might look for a diary that comes with a lock and key. Having a place to empty all your emotions honestly, without having to be worried about how others will react, can do wonders for your stress level and for helping you better understand the sources of some of your problems.

Remember: You're allowed to have needs as a kid, and you're not bad or wrong for being honest about that. In fact, you're incredibly brave. The next time you're thinking you "should" or "shouldn't" feel a certain way about all of this, remember that it's okay and normal to feel ALL of it. Both/and.

SCHOOL

Who doesn't have questions about school? It's a whole world in itself—classes, grades, friends, bullies, awesome teachers and staff (and not-so-awesome teachers and staff). . . . And when you're transitioning to middle and high school, there's a whole new set of rules and experiences to take in!

School can be a roller coaster of highs and lows. But it's good to remember through all your concerns that MILLIONS of other young people have gone through them too. That's a whole lot of people who can relate to any of your worries or fears!

Here are some ground rules about school: You should be able to feel safe and respected there, just as you are. And you should be able to find encouragement to pursue your dreams. Whether or not you feel like that's the case for you right now, read on to find some answers about how you too can best navigate school.

Content note: *In this chapter we will have honest discussions about when we don't feel safe in our schools, including when schools promote transphobia against trans students as well as the epidemic of gun violence in US schools.*

BRAVE BEGINNINGS

> **QUESTION:** I've seen a lot of movies and shows about middle and high school, and it always seems sort of terrifying. Will school actually be like that? Because I don't know what to expect and that's all I've seen.

School is very rarely like what we see on television. *Life* is very rarely like what we see on television.

Shows and movies are meant to capture our attention. They show us super popular people and super loners. They portray the kid who is the most brilliant and the one who seems like they know nothing. The truth is, most of us will experience being a little bit of all of those—at times having friends, other times being on our own, and feeling super smart in some situations and then less so in others. There will be so many opportunities for us to try on new hats as we do new things, find ourselves in new roles and places, and move through the seasons of our lives.

You will meet new people and maybe become lifelong friends. And you will meet people you may never want to see again. You will have teachers you love, and teachers who make your eyeballs want to fall out from boredom. You will have classes where you are great and excel and classes you struggle through. There is no one experience that is true about middle and high school. They're places to have many experiences and to learn about ourselves as we go through them. They're the places to discover things about you as you go. And if you're down for that ride, you'll do just fine. Always remember: If you're terrified, then everyone else probably is too, whether they're honest with you about it or not!

QUESTION: Have you ever been the new kid at school? What tips do you have for starting at a new school where you don't know anyone?

Oh boy have I! I was the new kid at a school ELEVEN times. Yup. That is almost a new school every year for my entire school career.

My dad was in the US Navy, and his job required us to move around very often. I would be lying if I said it was always easy. It was certainly simpler when I was younger, and making friends was as straightforward as walking up to a strange kid and offering them one of my cookies. But this process got trickier as I got older and attended schools where I felt so different from the other kids.

One of the biggest adjustments I had to make was leaving California and going to school in Pittsburgh, Pennsylvania. My Californian schools had a totally different culture than my new school, and I felt like a strange monster. I was different, and the biggest lesson I had to learn was being okay with being different and then finding other kids who also felt different and getting to know them.

It may take some time to find the people and groups you feel comfortable with. Be patient. Join groups that interest you. Don't waste a single second trying to "fit in" with other people: It keeps you from meeting your "right fit" people, the ones who will like you for you.

Again, it may be a bit rocky at first. You may find that you have intense feelings as you adjust to your new school. Allow yourself to experience all of the various and messy feelings you have, because they're all normal: excitement, fear, anxiety, confusion, hopefulness, loneliness, and more.

And remember that everyone will be new to someplace at some point in life. For example, in college, everyone is entering a new beginning. Everyone will be a new person when they start a new job. Everyone will be the new friend when connecting with a group of people who are already friends. Life is about letting go of old things and letting new things arrive—it's all part of being human.

Wanting to feel like we belong is natural, and sometimes it can take time. Be gentle with yourself as you explore the new terrain of your school and city. Remember that this can be the beginning of a new adventure where you get to share your remarkable fabulous self with a brand-new group of people. Aren't they lucky!

FITTING IN

QUESTION: Going to school makes me feel stupid. It's hard to concentrate and I don't get good grades. What's the point?

First and most importantly: You, my friend, are not stupid, and it stinks that school is making you feel that way. I promise it's not true.

Did you know that there are all different types of learners? There are kids who learn best by reading instructions, kids who do better looking at visual materials, and kids who shine when they can interact with physical things—say, a model of the solar system—and learn about it through physical touch and exploration.

Our schools are often set up to privilege certain types of learners over others, usually focusing on those who learn by reading and listening. This means some students are left struggling in traditional school settings. But it doesn't mean anyone is "stupid"—it means we need more creative and accessible teaching methods to suit the needs of many different students, and we need to make sure schools and teachers have the money and support they need to make it happen.

It's also useful to note that human brains are not one-size-fits-all. In other words, our brains don't all operate in the same way. The diverse ways people's brains respond to the world around us and help us process information is called **neurodiversity**. Imagine how boring the world would be if all our brains worked exactly the same!

As for not being able to concentrate, there are many different reasons why kids can't concentrate in school. This can include—but is not limited to—having upsetting things going on in their families; learning disabilities like **ADHD**, **dyslexia**, and **dyscalculia**; and not feeling physically and/or emotionally safe due to bullying.

I encourage you to think more about which parts of school are most difficult for you, and then talk to a safe adult about what to do. Schools often have teachers who can create Individualized Education Programs, or **IEPs**, to help students learn in the ways that best work for them. Because we all have unique ways our particular brilliance shows up, and we all deserve an educational experience that helps us shine!

> **QUESTION:** I love the learning part of school. I get really good grades and have started taking some advanced classes. But I also worry a LOT about making sure I have the best grades possible. When I get an A- or a B+ it really upsets me. Is it normal to feel that way?

Oh friend, it sounds like you may be struggling with **perfectionism**. Perfectionism is when someone wants to do well, to the point that they push themself to be perfect and judge themself harshly when they don't live up to their own unrealistic standards. It tends to be linked to anxiety and stems from fear of failing and of not being "good enough."

Perfectionism is a radical self-love issue. Humans are not perfect, and since you are a human, it stands to reason that you, darling, are not perfect.

Many people go through life as perfectionists, and it can cause lots of suffering. Making mistakes and getting things wrong are an essential part of learning. Given you love learning, being willing to be imperfect is going to be one of your greatest tools.

Of course, it's awesome you want to do well, get good grades, be successful, and pursue your dreams. But when stressing out about your (still fabulous, just not robotically flawless) grades starts impacting your mental health negatively and keeps you from experiencing the rest of life, like time with friends and family, it probably means you're being much too hard on yourself.

To combat this, I suggest you do a little exercise. Find a page in your journal or take out a sheet of paper and write down the following questions: "What do I fear? What is the worst thing that could happen if I don't get a 4.0? What will happen if I don't ace all of my exams?" Take some time and write down your answers. Maybe you are scared you'll get rejected from your dream college? Worried you won't be able to leave the town or city you're sick of when you turn eighteen? Concerned you'll let your family down? Locate the source of your fear. Oftentimes you will find that your fears are bigger than reality. If you get one bad grade, it will not keep you out of college forever. Our fears feel real but they are not necessarily telling us the truth about a situation. You, my dear, are driven, talented, and oh so very capable, and still, none of your achievements will make you more or less worthy or loveable.

You do not have to earn love through perfection. Trust that no matter what mistakes you make, you will still end up somewhere amazing that recognizes the unique gifts you bring. You've got this. You just need to give yourself some compassion, the same compassion you would offer an upset friend who was being too hard on themself.

This practice of compassion is one of my radical self-love tools I call **Give Yourself Some Grace**, and it is the most important tool in the radical self-love toolkit. Despite many years learning and teaching others about radical self-love, there are days when I am not "perfect" at loving myself radically.

Now, I could judge myself for not being perfect at this thing I have been studying for more than ten years, but not only is that not helpful, it's also unrealistic. We all live in a world where, from the time we wake up in the morning until we lie our heads on our pillows at night, we hear messages telling us we should have shinier hair and whiter teeth. We should weigh less, have more muscles, dress a certain way if we want to be popular, and make certain grades if we want to be considered smart or important. All day long we receive messages from media, businesses, schools, and other people that work to keep us feeling separated from our self-love. So of course there will be days when it feels difficult to remember how worthy and enough I am. But each time I recall all of the messages that make it so hard to practice radical self-love, I choose to give myself a break and let go of the need to be "perfect" at it.

Remember: No one is perfect, and radical self-love is not about perfection, it is about loving our whole selves, including our imperfections. You will have struggles in life; we all will. Talk with a friend about the goals you have that have nothing to do with grades. Remember all of the wonderful things about you that don't have anything to do with how you did in math class. No matter what your dreams for the future are, you need to be willing to make mistakes and get things wrong sometimes.

Perfection ultimately keeps us from fulfilling our biggest purpose, and you deserve to live your dreams, mistakes and all. It's good to take care of yourself, talk to a trusted adult about how you feel, and take breaks from schoolwork when you can. Doing fun things is crucial for our mental health. Your exciting and vibrant future is out there, cheering you on all the way.

QUESTION: If someone isn't popular in school, does that mean they're going to be an outcast as an adult?

NO! "Popularity" in middle and high school usually just means fitting into however your school defines "being like everybody else." It's its own curious phenomenon that has no bearing on what types of relationships we have in adulthood. As we get older, we don't have to focus quite so much on fitting in (conforming) with limited groups of people around us. We become much more interested in—and have more agency to be able to focus on—living *authentically* instead of trying to change ourselves into people we aren't. Part of growing up, especially after we leave high school and go out into the rest of the world as young adults, is to figure out what makes us *unique* and to find other people who share our interests and values. Some of the most interesting, creative, funny, smart, and successful adults I know weren't "popular" in school!

Also remember that there's a difference between being by yourself and being an outcast. Another big part of growing up is actually learning to get to know ourselves, to spend time with ourselves, to find peace and solitude in not always being around others so we can listen to our own needs and hearts. In other words, learning how to be okay on our own is important too. The more okay we are with being on our own, the more we will be able to know what we want from friendships and romantic relationships later in life.

I know it feels like school is going to last the rest of your life right now. But sooner than you realize, it will be a teeny-tiny chapter in the book of your life as you get older. The whole rest of the world is out there, waiting for you to make your mark on it!

QUESTION: I'm homeschooled, and sometimes people I meet ask why and act like it's weird. It makes me feel different and alone. Why do people act like this?

Hey, it's awful that folks are treating you like you're weird because you're not having the same school experience they are. If you haven't noticed yet, there's an issue that keeps coming up again and again in this book, and it's how terrible we humans are at dealing with differences.

Doing something different from the group doesn't mean you're automatically weird or less than them. It just means you're doing your own thing. It sounds like the kids who are putting you down are stuck in some oppressive "us" versus "them" thinking. They like feeling as if they're part of a group, and part of what helps them identify their own belonging in that group is to figure out who isn't in the group and then act as if they're superior. Again, it comes down to radical self-love: If they deeply felt their own inherent worthiness and enoughness, they wouldn't feel the need to seek outside validation from being in a group, nor would they feel the need to treat others badly.

People can be homeschooled for many reasons, including but not limited to religious beliefs, political beliefs, disability and illness, protection from extreme bullying, and conflicting schedules (like, for example, young people who have busy schedules as actors, singers, and professional athletes like gymnasts). So when you look at the bigger picture, homeschooling isn't weird at all. It's just different.

But if you're feeling alone, or don't feel like you're making the social connections you would like to, there're ways to connect with other kids who are homeschooled. Check out online resources by googling information about homeschooling. Consider making friends in your neighborhood, joining extracurricular groups if possible, and connecting online with other young people who have similar interests or cultural backgrounds.

You deserve friends who don't make you feel weird for being homeschooled. You deserve tons of joyful connection.

FREE FROM DANGER

> **QUESTION:** What can I do to stop people from bullying me? It makes going to school horrible.

Oh, friend. Everything you're feeling is entirely valid. And it really shouldn't be up to you to figure out how to "stop" the bullying, because no one deserves to be bullied. It's never okay to humiliate or talk down to someone, or to treat them with cruelty.

Bullying stems from other kids not being in touch with their own radical self-love. They don't feel good about themselves (because other people have made them feel bad about themselves, or they're experiencing other forms of pain), so they try to fill the hole by tearing down others. But hurting others to feel better about ourselves will never fill the hole that only radical self-love can fill. The more we see our own worth and value, the more we'll extend that belief out to others who are different from us. This is why tool number two for living radical self-love, **Curb Body Bad-Mouthing**, is so valuable. If we learn to stop judging and harshly speaking about our own bodies, we are more likely to recognize how cruel it is to do it to other bodies as well. (You can learn more about this tool at the back of the book.)

Of course, regardless of why kids become bullies, it absolutely does not make their behavior okay. Whenever someone is being bullied, I encourage them to find a safe adult and tell them that bullying is going on. It is important that they're *safe* adults, because adults can be bullies as well, including at school (see the next question below for more on this).

If you don't get help from the first adults you tell, or if you tell an adult and the bullying behavior persists, keep telling until you find an adult who will offer you support and care. Bullying is not okay, and you don't have to just take it.

> **QUESTION:** What do I do when the adults who are supposed to protect me at school aren't safe?

This is a good question, and one I'm sad you even have to ask. In a perfect world, adults—especially those at school—would always protect the young people in their care. Unfortunately, this is not always what happens.

All of us are imperfect humans. But some teachers and school administrators go beyond being imperfect and hold oppressive and harmful ideas, and that's never okay. This behavior can take many shapes, from teachers who sexually harass students or make inappropriate comments about their bodies, to adults who may hold racist, homophobic, or transphobic beliefs and share those in the school setting. But no matter the type of harm you're experiencing at school, it's not acceptable, and you can do things to challenge this.

First, as I said in the previous answer: Tell someone. And if they aren't helpful, tell someone else. You may have to tell several different people before you find someone to support you, and that's okay. Your safety is most important, and it is okay to bug adults to ensure they work to keep you safe. If you can't find a safe adult at your school to help advocate for you, you can absolutely talk to an adult outside school too.

Secondly, working in community is always a powerful way to take action. I'd suggest connecting with other students and seeing if other classmates are having similar issues. If so, consider writing down all your issues in a letter to the school administration (principal, superintendent, school board) or parent-teacher association. Keep documentation of the issues you are having with a specific adult, including dates, times, and the specific behavior or situation you experienced with the adult. Share this list with every safe adult you can think of until someone takes you seriously.

Later in the book, I'll share tips about protesting and taking action that can work in your school as well. Your education is an area of your life where you can step into your power and demand dignity and respect. I promise if you keep speaking your truth, someone is bound to listen.

> **QUESTION:** My sister is trans. Why do people care what bathroom she uses at school? It makes her really upset and feel like everyone doesn't see her for who she is.

First of all, you're an awesome sibling for caring so much about this hard thing your sister is going through. She's lucky to have such a loving family member in her corner.

If people at school are shaming her for using the bathroom that best suits her identity and needs, they are engaging in transphobia, which is fear and hatred against transgender people. This is completely unacceptable, and in the US was ruled illegal by the Fourth Circuit Court of Appeals in 2020 after a brave trans student named Gavin Grimm sued his school for anti-trans discrimination in 2015. In 2021, the US Department of Education also announced that trans kids should be legally protected from discrimination at school.

People who are transphobic against trans girls and women using the bathrooms they need often justify it by saying they are concerned about male predators going into girls' bathrooms. No good and decent people, including those of us who care about equality for trans people, think girls and women should be assaulted in bathrooms. Luckily for us all, this should not be a worry because first, trans girls are not males, and second, trans girls are not predators.

If we want to stop men from sexually harassing and assaulting girls and women, we should focus on that—which would mean taking sexual assault and sexism seriously—rather than hurting trans girls and women. Your sister deserves to be treated respectfully based on who she is, not based on fears of people she isn't. She can use some of the strategies we mentioned earlier about finding safety at school to demand respect and care in her school.

Here are some US-based resources your family can access to help you fight back against transphobia and discrimination:

- **Sylvia Rivera Law Project: https://srlp.org**
- **National Center for Transgender Equality's Youth & Students page: https://transequality.org/issues/youth-students**
- **Transgender Law Center's Youth Resources page: https://**

transgenderlawcenter.org/resources/youth

- GLSEN's Trans and GNC Voices page: https://www.glsen.org/supporting-trans-and-gnc-students
- Trans Lifeline (also in Canada): https://translifeline.org

QUESTION: Why does the United States have school shootings? Why don't kids in other countries have to deal with that?

I wish there was an easy answer to this question. If there were, it would mean we could have easily solved this issue, and many young people might still be alive today.

School shootings are just one devastating version of an even larger issue of gun violence in the US, and that problem is like an octopus with many tentacles. One of those tentacles is the United States' long-standing and unaddressed history of violence. As a nation founded on genocide against Native Americans and the enslavement of Africans, violence is sewn into the very fabric of American culture.

Another tentacle is patriarchy and sexism, which we discussed earlier in this book. The majority of school shootings are carried out by boys and young men, and US culture often tells boys that violence is the best and only way to deal with their emotions or solve their problems. This message we give boys and men is called **toxic masculinity**, and too often it leads to the use of violence to deal with everything from anger and grief to unresolved trauma.

But one of the longest, most frustrating tentacles of gun violence in the US is gun laws.

Patriarchy, sexism, toxic masculinity, and even histories of violence exist in countries around the world. The US is not an exception. However, most countries have gun control laws that restrict who has access to guns and ensure guns cannot easily end up in the hands of young people. In New Zealand, the country I live in, there has only been one mass school shooting. It occurred in 1923, when two students were killed, and six others were injured. Because New Zealand has laws about who can have a gun license and what kinds of guns can be sold to the public, mass shootings and school shootings are rare. This is true for pretty much every other country besides the US, which stands alone as a world outlier for mass shootings.

In fact, the US is currently the only country on earth that protects gun ownership in its constitution without any restrictions. It also has groups with lots of money and political power, called **lobbyists**, who work incredibly hard to keep politicians from voting for gun control. These people seem to believe that having uncontrolled access to guns will keep us safe, even when all the evidence proves that gun laws make us safer. Gun lobbyists also make lots of money from gun sales, so they've come to care more about their profits than protecting people's lives. However, every day both young people and adults all over the US build power through organizing and activism to challenge the gun lobbyists and bring about sensible gun control laws, such as through the organization March For Our Lives. Even though you shouldn't have to, I do believe that school shootings and gun violence are another issue where kids will lead us adults in creating a safer, more compassionate world.

FRIENDS

Friends are so important to have with us on this journey of life. Friends should be there to laugh with us, to support us when we're down, and to receive our help when they're down too. They're there to make incredible memories we'll remember forever.

At its best, friendship is a way to deeply know and care about each other in ways so big that we can feel like family. I mentioned this earlier in the Family section. I have friends who have helped me through some of the most difficult experiences in my life, like the death of my mother. My friends have also celebrated my biggest accomplishments, cheering me through graduations, new businesses, and even this book! Friendships can be some of the most important relationships we will have in our lifetime.

But it's also true that many friendships don't last a lifetime, that we can argue with our friends, and that some friendships will end. There are so many reasons why this happens, from being treated poorly to no longer having things in common, or because one person has to move away, and you gradually stop talking to each other. These situations, while hard emotionally, are also completely normal.

Ultimately, friendships are one of the most important experiences where we learn more about ourselves. Let's explore this idea more, as well as what it means to be a friend, have a friend, and understand friendship as you grow and change.

FINDING YOUR FOLKS

> **QUESTION:** How do I pick good friends?

Picking good friends is like picking good fruit. My mother used to tell me that when I went to the market, I should sniff the fruit and knock on it to see if it was firm or soft. Picking friends is similar. Now, I'm not telling you to knock on or sniff your friends! But I *am* saying you will need to do some work to know what you want and whether the friend is a good fit.

One of the first tips in picking good friends is remembering that friendship is a two-way street. Unfortunately, I've had times when I wanted to be friends with people who didn't really want to be friends with me. Sometimes I tried to force a friendship, and it never worked—in fact, it usually left me feeling awful. Trying to force a friendship usually meant trying to act like someone I was not. Pretending to like things I really didn't or pretending not to like things I really did. Basically, I was acting like someone other than the real me. I had to learn that the first key to good friendships is being friends with people who wanted to be friends with me—the real me.

Sometimes you can begin by looking at the qualities that make you a good friend: Are you silly and fun? Great at games? A good listener? And then consider what qualities you would like to have more of in your life. Maybe you like being around someone who is smart, and you can both study together, or maybe they are generous like you and you both share your school lunches with each other. Perhaps you choose a person you can just hang out with for hours and not do anything specific. All friendships are about giving and receiving, and maybe most importantly, joy, connection, and fun.

Picking friends is about knowing what makes us feel connected and brings us joy. Once you know what you like in a friend and what kind of friend you are, you can start matching your list to the experiences you're having with others your age. I'm not suggesting you have a checklist on which to check people off, but it does help to know what kind of energy you like so you can spend more time around people who have those qualities, as well as people who will bring out the best qualities in you when you're around them. And that way you can end up with the best fruit (friend) for you!

Lastly, fruit takes time to ripen. So do friendships. You may not know whether a person is a good fit for friendship immediately. That's okay. Take your time and get to know a person and let that person get to know you. Only with patience can the juiciest, sweetest true friendships grow.

QUESTION: What is a good way to make friends?

Making friends can feel like risky business. *What if they don't like me? What if they think I'm weird?* All of these are questions that can come up when we're trying to meet people. But when we're connected to our radical self-love, it helps us feel less scared when we're inviting others to get to know us too. Because if we already know how worthy and amazing we are just by being our most authentic selves, we won't feel as pressured to change ourselves into whoever we think others want us to be.

Since friendships are social relationships, you have to be willing to be (at least a little) social to make friends. An important part of this is figuring out where to meet people. You may meet people at your school, through extracurricular activities, or at your church, mosque, or synagogue. In the process of meeting people, you'll often need to step up and start a conversation. You may have to ask someone you don't know their name and some questions about who they are. You can repeat back something interesting that you learned about them in your conversation and figure out if you have anything in common. You may also see someone doing something you like and ask if you can do it with them, like playing a game or watching a show.

None of these things guarantee that you'll make friends. But they *will* increase the chance of meeting people that you like and want to spend time with. The key is to put yourself out there and look for connections—the more people you meet, the more people you are likely to feel a genuine interest in. And with a little bit of effort on both parts, a gorgeous friendship can bloom!

QUESTION: How do you know your friends are your friends because they need you or because they really do like you?

I am going to share one of my favorite words with you: **reciprocity**! Reciprocity is like the magic fairy dust of friendship: Having reciprocity in a friendship means that both people make it work. Both people put in effort and care and attention to make it blossom. If you have reciprocity, you won't be left wondering if your friend is using you because they need you—your friend will show you through their actions that they really like you and value you in their life.

Friends who really like you are your friend even if you don't have money or gifts to give them. True friends help you when you're down or having a rough time. They want to support you just as you support them. If your friendships don't have reciprocity, it might be worth asking yourself if you're okay with how you're being treated. If you feel like you are not okay, consider talking to your friend about it. Perhaps make a list of what they could do that would make you feel like your friendship has more reciprocity and share it with them. If they are a true friend, they will want to work with you to make sure the friendship meets the needs of both of you.

> **QUESTION:** How do I know if I can trust my friends or other people? How do we come to trust people?

Trust is one of those things that everyone has different ideas about. Some people will tell you they only trust people when they have earned trust or proven themselves. Others say they trust everyone until they are given a reason not to trust.

I probably fall somewhere in the middle: I believe that humans are good people who sometimes make mistakes, which can make trusting them difficult. If you start from the idea that people usually have good intentions, though also are capable of causing harm, you can offer them a certain amount of trust in the beginning of the relationship. As time goes on and you experience kindness and reciprocity in the relationship, you can begin offering more trust to your friends or others.

For example, I would hope that you wouldn't give all your allowance money to a person you just met. You wouldn't be able to tell how much you could trust them just yet, after all. But if you've known them for a long time and you have confidence that they will pay you back, you may be willing to share with them. Trust grows with time and care. In fact, I think trust is more valuable than money.

To get the right balance of trust, you must start off with good boundaries. Revisit our conversation about boundaries earlier in the book and explore what sort of boundaries you may need to set in the beginning of your friendship. Maybe that means not sharing about certain family experiences or waiting to share something that is truly important until you feel like you know them better. You will know your friends are trustworthy because they honor your boundaries.

I asked one of my brilliant friends and podcast host Natalie Lue if, as a mom, she had any thoughts on this question. She shared that when her daughter felt confused and doubtful about certain friendships, Natalie would ask her to think about other friends and people she felt good about herself around. She asked her which friends she trusted and had her compare those friendships with the ones she was feeling doubtful about. This advice helped her daughter recognize what was and was not working in her friendships.

Good friends genuinely want you to be happy and seek to include you. And they make you feel cared for and respected. If those things are present over time, someone may indeed be a person you can truly trust.

A SOMETIMES-ROCKY ROAD

> **QUESTION:** My best friend said he doesn't want to be my best friend anymore and it really hurt my feelings. Why do some friendships grow apart when you get into middle and high school? Why is making and keeping friends so hard?

First, let me say I'm really sorry that your friend doesn't want to be your best friend anymore. I can imagine that it really hurts.

When we have people that we care about deeply and the relationship changes, it can be very painful. I wish I could tell you why your best friend doesn't want to be your best friend anymore, but I don't have that superpower. What I can tell you is that humans are always changing, and so are our needs and wants. And as we change, our relationships inevitably change.

For example, when I was younger, I had "friends" who weren't always kind to me, or who were into things I just didn't enjoy. But I stayed friends with them because I wanted everyone to like me. I thought that if everyone liked me, I would never be alone. (Now that I'm older, I realize that everyone doesn't have to like me. And being alone isn't always so bad.)

As I changed, though, I realized that those people didn't match who I was becoming. That didn't mean they were bad people. And it didn't mean I was a bad person. It just meant that we were becoming different people. And it's okay to change.

Imagine trying to wear the shoes you had when you were five. It would be very uncomfortable trying to squeeze your big foot into that shoe now. Not only do our feet grow, but our ideas, thoughts, and personalities also shift and change over time, which may mean that our relationships don't fit anymore. And that's okay. It's also okay to be sad and miss your friend and still honor that both of you are changing and—for now—are on different paths. You can also hold the possibility your paths may come back together at some point.

QUESTION: What should I do when two people I was best friends with have become very close and are leaving me out?

My first question back to you is, have you asked them? Sometimes we experience things, and we are too scared to ask our friends about what's going on.

It's possible that your two friends are leaving you out. It's also possible that they are building a relationship and it *feels* like they are leaving you out. Speaking up about how you are feeling is an opportunity to explore what is really going on. But you can only find out if you ask.

Sometimes we expect the people we care about to read our minds, figure out the thing that will make us happy, and then do that specific thing. "She didn't invite me to go to the movies last week," we might think to ourselves, all the while forgetting that we said we had a ton of homework and needed to stay home and complete it. But now we think our friends are leaving us out.

That's unfair to them. Because again, no one has mind-reading superpowers. The best way to know why your friends aren't including you is to share how you are feeling and ask your friends what's going on. If you want to be included more in this three-way friendship, then you, my dear, are going to have to ask for what you need and have an honest, open, vulnerable conversation. Of course, having this conversation does not necessarily mean your friends will begin to include you in the way you want. I can't promise that they will even be nice to you when you share how you are feeling (trust me, I wish I had a *make all the people nice* wand!). If your friends don't respond by including you more often, that may be a sign that they are not great friends for you, and it may be time to explore making new friendships. You can do this by participating in fun activities that bring you joy and connect you to others. You can spend time building your connections with other people who make you feel good. Revisit the question on how to make friends. But before we get to any of that, you, friend, are going to have to talk to your two pals. It all starts there. Check out the back of the book where I share my **Community Conversation Agreements** that can help you have a conversation guided by radical self-love. Try it. I promise, no matter how it turns out, it will pay off in the end.

First, let me say that it's a sign of a good friend to want to help your friends when they are struggling. That means you are a kind and compassionate person.

It's important, in our desire to help people, that we always ask first. Helping requires consent. Sometimes when people are struggling, they might want their friends to give them advice about what they should do. Other times, they might just want their friends to listen to what's on their mind and feel like their friends care about them and what they're going through. A good way to practice consent when your friend is struggling is to ask them how they're feeling and what they need from you. Have your friends talked to you about how they're struggling? Have they asked you for something specific? If they don't want to talk about it, you might not have their consent to offer advice.

Sometimes what we need most is a good listener. Someone who is willing to listen to our struggles and lovingly support us without doing anything, just letting us know we're not alone. Other times, we may need that help or advice. Keep this in mind when your friend is struggling, and make sure to ask them what they might need before launching into advice. They may just need you to listen quietly.

There will also be times when our friends have challenges that are bigger than we have the skills to help with. We must be honest with ourselves about that, since trying to help when we don't know how could end up doing more harm than good and can deplete our energy. Checking in with yourself and making sure you are not sacrificing yourself to help your friend is important. Caring for ourselves is necessary if we are going to offer true care to others. If you feel that your friend is in danger of hurting themself or hurting someone else, you should *always* seek support from a trusted adult.

QUESTION: Can a friendship be mended? Will my friendships last forever?

The answer is yes . . . and sometimes no. Friendships are a partner dance. Both people must be willing to do the mending.

Like anything else, friendships take work. And it takes commitment from both parties to work at it. For example, there are times we may have done something that really hurt our friend, and they don't feel like they can forgive us. Depending on what happened, you may owe your friend an apology. There may also be times when your friend does something that upsets or hurts you, and you feel like they owe you an apology.

An honest apology can go a long way in mending friendships. A good apology means you're willing to own up to what you did without blaming others or making excuses. It lets you express that you're sorry for how your actions may have hurt the other person and offer a plan for how you'll do things differently in the future. If you can do this, you may find it really helps the friendship heal.

Unfortunately, there may be times you feel like you are owed an apology and your friend refuses. Your friend may not see the issue how you see it or may be unwilling to apologize. This may make you feel angry, frustrated, or even hurt. All of those feelings are valid, and you cannot force someone to apologize. You can think about the qualities you want in a friend, like someone who says they're sorry if they hurt you, and decide if this person is someone you want to keep around as a friend. Later on in this chapter we will take a look at the qualities of a good friend. I happen to know one of them is that good friends are willing to be accountable for their actions.

However, apologies may not always fix what's broken. Think about something in your life that has been broken. Perhaps it's a toy, a bike, or your mom's good china you dropped while doing the dishes. (I did that once . . . YIKES.) Everything cannot always be fixed, and that's okay. There will be times when mending can't happen because the pieces simply do not fit together anymore. Earlier in this chapter we talked about how friends can grow apart. While that can be a hard experience to adjust to, and it may take some time to heal and move forward, that doesn't mean anyone has done anything wrong. It just means we humans change. Mending a friendship is possible, but only if both people want to mend it. Sometimes it's better to focus our energy on allowing space in our lives for new friends who better fit with who we've become, and with whom we can have new experiences. It's okay to honor a friendship for what it was and let it go. You'll always have the memories.

PARTING WAYS

QUESTION: What kind of friendships should you let go of?

Time for a visualization exercise! Let's practice Natalie Lue's suggestion she gave her daughter. Take a moment and think about the person or people you feel most loved by and cared about. What are the characteristics of those relationships? Write them down if you'd like. Then think about the friendship or friendships you're wondering if you should let go of. How do those make you feel? Write down five to seven of the first things that come to mind (focus on one friendship at a time when you do this). Is this list filled with positive things, negative things, or a mix of both?

Now check out the following list from my book *Celebrate Your Body*. It's called "Twenty Qualities that Make a Good Friend," which I created after collecting the top ideas from a bunch of my friends. How many of these items describe the friendship you're unsure of?

Twenty Qualities that Make a Good Friend

1. A good friend doesn't want to hurt your feelings.
2. A good friend says sorry when they hurt you.
3. A good friend wants to have you around.
4. A good friend wants to help you make more good friends.
5. A good friend encourages you.

6. A good friend is kind to you and others.

7. A good friend listens to you.

8. A good friend wants to help, even if they are not sure what to do or say in the moment.

9. A good friend admits when they are wrong.

10. A good friend likes it most when you're being your truest self.

11. A good friend doesn't gossip about you or others.

12. A good friend doesn't ask you to choose between you and other friends.

13. A good friend doesn't talk behind your back.

14. A good friend inspires you to do your best.

15. A good friend is honest.

16. A good friend stands up for you and their other friends.

17. A good friend tells you if something is dangerous or harmful.

18. A good friend laughs with you, not at you.

19. A good friend makes time for you.

20. A good friend tries to make you feel better.

How did your friendship stack up? When the things that matter to you the most are not present in that relationship, you know it's time to leave, which is not an easy process. And it is possible to really love and care for someone *and* to know that they don't meet the characteristics of the kinds of friends you want. This can be a very painful realization, to both hold that love for someone while also knowing they're not a good friend for you. But your love for someone else should never be prioritized over the love you deserve to give yourself. It's okay to let go of their friendship.

My reasons to end a friendship may be different from yours, and so you will have to consider for yourself what sort of actions feel like reasons to end a friendship. However, I will say that you should never have to accept violence, demeaning behavior, people who put you down, who are cruel to you, or people who ask you to harm yourself or harm others. Those are not behaviors of people who care about you, and those are relationships you should always leave.

As I've mentioned before, having an honest conversation together is a mature way to find out if the friendship truly needs to end. Once you've had that, you can walk away knowing you did your best. That's a big deal!

QUESTION: How do I end a friendship?

There is no one "correct" way to end a friendship, and how to do so can change depending on why the friendship is ending.

Honesty is usually the best way to deal with this situation. There may be some hurt on one or both sides—your soon-to-be-ex-friend may have harmed you in a way you feel can't be mended, or they might be upset that your friendship is ending, or view what happened differently than you do.

This is all normal. It's important to honor what's in your heart and try to keep as calm as possible. When you talk to them, you can practice communicating using "I" statements, which will help you have the conversation without blaming the other person. If you are using an "I" statement, you might say, "I felt angry when you weren't speaking to me last week." By saying it this way, you're owning your feelings about their actions without making your friend bad or wrong. You may also want to give them a chance to respond without interrupting them, and ask that they do the same for you.

These communication tips can help the conversation happen without becoming a big argument. But no matter how nicely you talk to them, it's likely that the conversation will be at least a little uncomfortable, and that's okay. You can use our **Community Conversation Agreements** at the end of this book to guide the conversation and explain where you're coming from.

There will be times, whether you have a conversation with your friend or not, when your friendship just naturally comes to an end. Think of it like a candle being (carefully) allowed to burn until it's out. If you're already drifting apart and don't have much in common anymore, it might make more sense to simply go your own ways. Listen to your intuition for what feels right for your situation. And when a friendship does end, honor the bravery it took inside yourself to undergo such a hard but necessary thing.

GROWING UP

Pssst: Here's a secret—we're never done growing up! There's always more to learn and discover about ourselves and the world around us. But there is a significant shift that happens from childhood to adolescence and on to adulthood— that period of time that you're living right now. Some of my biggest questions during this time were about what I would eventually do as a career when I became an adult, how I would manage in college, and if I was destined to have some of the same struggles I saw my family have.

My answers didn't arrive overnight, but they eventually came because I was willing to keep asking and looking for answers, just like you. If you find yourself with big questions like *Who am I really?* and *What is my future going to look like?*, that makes total sense. After all, this is a time of both great excitement and stress. Let's see if we can find some answers together!

WHO I AM, WHO I'LL BE

> **QUESTION:** How do I know exactly who I am? When does that become clear?

Oh honey, I'm sorry to be the one to inform you, but . . . the answer is maybe never. The truth is that humans are complicated, complex, messy, gorgeous, divine beings. And the work to figure out who we are to ourselves, to others, to the world, is the work of our entire lifetimes. I think that work is much easier if we first and foremost see ourselves as radical love.

Maybe everything else is just a big juicy puzzle we came to earth to practice putting together. The famous writer Walt Whitman once said, "I am large. I contain multitudes." It seems to me, Walt was reminding us that we are all likely to be many different things throughout our lives. Some of those things will be delightful, fascinating, exceptional parts of identity. Others will be imperfect, maybe a little scary, or even sad to face. Yet, all of it is you and all of you is loveable. To uncover all the elements of who we are will take all of the years you are on the planet and like a never-ending bowl of spaghetti, you may still never get to the bottom. Nevertheless, take your time and enjoy each bite of this delicious life, my friend!

This is a question that even us so-called grown-ups ask ourselves! It might help to first explore what we mean when we say "grown up." People often define being a grown-up simply by their age (that's the legal definition of being an adult, after all). But there are many adult-aged people whose behavior is . . . less than grown up. So being a true grown-up also has a lot to do with **emotional maturity**—being able to understand and regulate our emotions, as well as communicate compassionately with other people.

TV and movies often make it seem like being a grown-up has to do with certain life milestones: getting married, having kids, buying a house, and working at a fancy job. But that's only some of what adults do, and not everyone even wants those things. For example, there are adults who decide never to get married. There are adults for whom buying a house is financially out of reach. And there are adults who don't have children, whether because they don't want kids or medically cannot have them, they can't afford to, or they're trying to help the environment by not making more people.

Being a grown-up, you'll discover, is less about achieving certain types of milestones or being a certain age and more about developing the life skills you'll need to take care of yourself and others.

What are some life skills you'll need to be a grown-up? Being able to communicate your feelings respectfully and with compassion for others, as I mentioned above. Learning how to sustain yourself through cooking for yourself, doing your own laundry, cleaning your living area, and attending to your personal hygiene and wellness (like all those showers and consistent bedtimes we talked about before!). Getting a job or starting a business to earn money so you can stay on top of your rent and other bills is also a big one.

However, these skills can be complicated by things like disability (in which case, you may need help from others or **accommodations** to do these tasks), or by oppression, since things like job discrimination, being paid less due to your gender and/or race, and unequal access to educational and career opportunities still prevent life being truly equitable for everyone. And these realities don't make you any less of a grown-up even if you find yourself struggling with them.

One of the most rewarding parts of becoming a grown-up is slowly but surely trusting your radical self-love and realizing you can be there for yourself. You are your own best friend and advocate. You know yourself and trust yourself to make good decisions, have healthy boundaries, and live your best life. In a way, you become a parent to yourself, protecting yourself and nurturing yourself instead of only trying to please everyone around you. And that is the type of grown-up everyone has the potential to become if we aim for it.

> **QUESTION:** How am I supposed to know what I want to "be" when I grow up? What if I change my mind about my career later on? What job options are even out there?

Testing out new things, changing our minds, and trying other things is all part of life—and of adulthood especially. Having the rest of our lives figured out when we're ten or twelve or fifteen or twenty, twenty-five, or even forty-five (like me) would be unrealistic and even concerning!

Life is a beautiful adventure with twists and turns and possibilities. You have time to figure out what you're passionate about, what you're good at, and what new skills and interests you might develop. And lots of people start out with one life path or college major, or build a whole career, and then change their plans later. I have had five different careers so far, and I will probably have more!

If you want to learn more about possible job options, I suggest making a list of things you're good at, things you want to try, and things you're interested in. Then go online and look up careers that use those skills and that focus on those topics. See what kind of training programs and/or degrees people typically need to do them. You have a lot of time to explore, but there's no harm in thinking about it early if you're curious!

QUESTION: What does success mean? How do I know if I'm successful? When can I ever be satisfied with what I've accomplished?

Whoa, friend! Are you ten or are you forty-five? This is a question that many of us spend our entire lives asking.

We live in a world that tells us success is outside of us. Maybe it's about how much money we make, or if we have the coolest job or the biggest house, or the fastest, shiniest car. But I know a lot of people who have all those things and still do not feel successful or like it's enough. I think this is because feeling like we are "enough" is not about our outside achievements.

Radical self-love says that we arrive on this planet already enough. Worthy enough to be loved, special enough to be cared for, human enough to be treated with respect and dignity. There is nothing we have to do to earn it—we are enough simply by existing. And if we're already enough, then success is whatever we do with our lives when we truly understand this.

We get to define success based on what makes us happy, what brings us joy, and how we contribute to the joy and happiness of other humans. And by that definition, it doesn't matter how much money we have, what kind of car we drive, or what kind of job we choose. What matters most is that we love ourselves, and we let that love guide how we show up in the world. Then, no matter what we do, we'll be successful.

HARD WORK OR HEART WORK

QUESTION: What's the hardest part about growing up? Or, what was the hardest part for you, and how did you overcome it?

Honey, that is a whole other book I will be writing later! There is an expression called *"building the plane as you fly it"* that I think perfectly encompasses what growing up can be like. People say this phrase to describe what it's like to learn something and try to practice it at the same time.

Just imagine what it would be like to stand on an airplane wing with a hammer and nails while trying to hammer that wing on as it soars through the sky, all without plummeting into the ocean! NO THANK YOU! I'd rather not. All jokes aside, growing up can be hard because we're learning massive amounts of lessons and trying to live what we learn all at the same time. It can feel scary, unnerving, and exhilarating.

The most difficult part of growing up for me was unlearning what I believed about myself and creating new beliefs. I used to believe I needed people to like me to be loved. I used to believe my grades, friends, and hard work could fix the challenges I had at home. If I were just smart enough, funny enough, and liked enough, maybe my mom would stop using drugs. Then maybe she would be able to love and take care of me . . . because I had proved I was good enough.

I have lots of compassion and sweetness for the little Sonya who had those beliefs. I understand what made her think those things. But growing up taught me that love was something I had to give myself. And when I gave myself lots of love, more love found its way to me. I didn't have to be perfect or get the best grades or make the most friends to deserve it. I had to learn that my mother's challenges were not my fault, and they didn't mean that I did anything wrong or wasn't smart, funny, or liked enough to change her.

I learned we can't change other people. We can only be ourselves. I had to let myself be imperfect, silly, loving Sonya, and when I allowed that Sonya to exist, things got so much easier.

You are super lucky because you don't have to wait until you're a grown-up to learn all these lessons. You're reading about these lessons right now, in this book, and you get to carry them with you as you get older.

Does that mean growing up won't be hard? Nope! I cannot grant you that wish (no matter how much I want to). However, when we are connected to our radical self-love, growing up gets to be just as fun and wild and beautiful as it is hard, and *that* is a ride totally worth taking.

QUESTION: I'm scared to grow up because I am very attached to my family and I'm afraid to leave them.

You must have a very sweet family to feel so close to them. And I think this question is another invitation for us to redefine "growing up." Growing up doesn't mean you have to leave your family behind.

There are lots of cultures where people grow up and get married and still live in the family home. There are many different family structures that exist—such as multigenerational homes, where different generations of a family live together—and other ways we can continue to connect with our families while still living our adult lives.

And there are ways we can stay in touch with our families no matter how far away we are physically or geographically. Leaving geographically doesn't mean we have to leave emotionally. We can still call our families, video chat with them, send them things in the mail, and visit them on holidays, if possible, or other times too.

It's also important not to lose sight of the fact that growing up and gaining independence as an adult means there will be so many choices you'll be able to make for yourself! So many things you'll get to see and do that you haven't yet. A whole adventure awaits! While it's completely understandable for you to hold some fear, I hope you'll also give yourself permission to feel some of the excitement bubbling up inside you as you look toward your grown-up future.

QUESTION: Is being an adult better than being a kid?

The answer to this question depends on so many different things! For instance, do you like your life now as a kid? For many people who went through lots of challenges as kids, like bullying, not being accepted for who they are, hating where they live, or surviving abuse, growing up and having way more control over their lives as an adult is an exciting, hopeful, joyous thing.

At the same time, adulthood comes with lots of responsibilities. In some ways you have to be your own parent (as I mentioned earlier) and do things you might not want to, like going to the dentist and eating veggies sometimes. You also have to learn how to make money and pay your bills, which is not a joy, let me tell you!

Maybe we don't have to compare them at all. Being a kid can be an awesome part of living, and so can being an adult. You can find ways to keep your kid-self alive inside your grown-up self, the one who loves bike rides, playing with friends, and telling scary stories. That way, you never have to choose between the two.

QUESTION: I am a fourteen-year-old girl with cerebral palsy, and I am struggling to remember that there is nothing wrong with me. It doesn't help when I'm out in public, online, or even at school and somebody asks, "What's wrong with you?" because I never really know what to say. Can you help me? What do you say if or when someone asks you what is wrong with you?

ASK AN EXPERT: My friend Keah Brown is a journalist, author, and creator of the hashtag campaign #DisabledAndCute. She even wrote a book called *The Pretty One*, exploring what it means to be disabled and Black in a world geared toward non-disabled people. Keah is smart, confident, and disabled. I thought she would be just the right person to answer this question.

First, I want you to immediately know that there is absolutely nothing wrong with you. You're fourteen years old and have your whole life ahead of you. I already know how cheesy that sounds, but it's true. I was fourteen many years ago and I remember that everything felt so urgent and like such a big deal—and in many ways, it was and it is. Fourteen is when you start to take time to figure out who you are and what you want in life. So many things will shift and change for you between fourteen and thirty-one (which is my age). But the one thing that will never change is the fact that there is absolutely nothing wrong with you.

As disabled people, we have had to adapt to a world that is not designed for us, and with that comes questions, often inappropriate ones and even from people with the best of intentions. I didn't know how to answer them at fourteen either, but I can tell you what I know now. When someone asks me, "What's wrong with you?" or "What happened to you?" I take a deep, centering breath and say, "Nothing."

Now, depending on the day and the person asking, I follow up with one of two things: Either, "I have cerebral palsy. It's a neurological disability that impacts my body, but I'm fine." Or, I make up some fantastical story about an accident or fight I got into that left me with the limp they see me walking with and a right hand that doesn't look like my left. Despite how exhausting the question is, the fantastical stories are fun to make up because not everyone who asks is owed the truth. The rude or invasive people usually get the fantastical story and the polite questioners get the truth.

However, I hope you understand that no one outside of your team of medical professionals is entitled to know your medical history just because they're curious. You can and should always reserve the right to decline to answer that question. You are not required to teach anyone anything. You are a person first, not a lesson to learn. So the next time someone tries to make you believe that your disability means there is something wrong with you—the next time someone asks, "What is wrong with you?" I hope you remember these words: *Absolutely nothing.*

A RADICAL LOVE FUTURE

QUESTION: My parents are divorced, and I don't want to end up like them. What are some signs that someone would be good or bad to date in the future? Does everyone just break up in the end?

I'm going to answer the second part of your question first: It's true that some couples do get divorced. Many others break up before they get to the point where they might've gotten married. But not everyone breaks up in the end. Perhaps most importantly, though—staying together isn't always the best answer. It can be healthier for people to break up when they don't get along anymore or don't have enough in common so that they can live their best, fullest lives (whether single or with someone else). Would you want to be stuck being with someone you didn't get along with, or who was mean to you, or who didn't respect you, for the rest of your life? I hope your answer is no!

Given that you said your parents are divorced, it's likely that you had to witness their breakup. I'm sure that experience was pretty darn stressful for you. And it makes sense that it might've impacted how you view love and family. After all, if your own family had to go through the pain of divorce, how are you supposed to trust that it won't happen to you when you grow up? These are all super normal and common feelings to have in your situation.

Despite how very upsetting breakups and divorce can be, humans would be much worse off if we were forced to stay together when we don't want to. Your parents ultimately made a healthy choice by getting divorced, right? And remember, just because a relationship ends doesn't mean it was a failure. Sometimes we are with people to learn lessons about ourselves and life, and if we have learned those lessons, the relationship was successful even if it didn't last. After all, your parents got you as a result of their relationship, and that's worth forever celebrating!

As for your question about signs that someone would be good or bad to date, everyone should think a lot about this before they start dating, and also throughout their lives. It's so important that we be able to identify **red flags** (things that don't seem quite right and are warning us to be careful, or even stop) and **green flags** (things that feel good to us and our intuition and encourage us to keep going).

Red flags in a relationship (whether it's a romantic relationship or not) are those things that can be considered toxic and/or abusive: someone trying to control you, not respecting your boundaries, putting you down and making you feel bad about yourself, refusing to apologize for bad behavior, apologizing for things they do wrong but then not doing better, physically harming you in any way or threatening to do so, and more. Green flags can include someone having emotional maturity, treating you with respect and compassion, respecting your boundaries, doing thoughtful things for you, and recognizing that you are your own person with your own valid thoughts and feelings.

It's important to note here that abusive relationships don't usually start out as full-blown abusive. Most people wouldn't agree to date someone who treated them horribly up front! This is why it's so important to pay attention to red flags. Relationships can sometimes become more and more abusive after a beginning period of **"love bombing,"** which is when someone gives another person lots of compliments, attention, or gifts to get that person to love and trust them, then starts acting in mean, cruel, or scary ways.

Remember, there is *no* excuse for treating romantic partners abusively, including emotionally. Always listen to your intuition, and don't be afraid to get advice from a trusted friend or relative about how a date or romantic partner is treating you. Having a healthy, happy relationship doesn't mean that you'll never disagree, or even argue, about something. But it does mean you'll be able to communicate with each other in respectful, safe ways, and that you'll see your relationship as being part of a team that works together, instead of taking sides.

You should both be creating a relationship that is **interdependent**, which means you each have your own lives as individual, unique people, but also that you add to each other's lives as you build your life together. Some therapists refer to this idea as both of you walking down a road together, each on your own separate path, while holding hands.

Can you think of any adult relationships in your life that are healthy and make you feel happy and secure? If so, what are some things about those relationships that you admire? Despite what you may see from your own divorced parents, these types of relationships are out there. And you deserve nothing less.

QUESTION: Why do adults not believe in us?

Because sometimes, adults are ridiculous. Adults tend to think we know everything and that kids know less than us just because you're younger. This is called **adultism**, and it's a form of ageism. (There is also ageism against older people, such as assuming older people won't be able to understand technology in the workplace—it works both ways!)

While it's true that kids' brains and the rest of their bodies aren't done developing yet, and it's necessary for adults to make various decisions to help guide younger people, that doesn't mean that kids don't have awesome ideas; don't understand their own identities, feelings, or experiences; or shouldn't be trusted. Quite the contrary— kids are innovating and changing our world every day! I, for one, am a huge admirer of the power and brilliance of young people. This adult totally believes in you and wants you to believe in yourself!

QUESTION: Why is it that every day in the world there seems to be more problems? Why do people not seem to care about it?

As unlikely as it may seem, there have always been problems and horrors across the world since humans existed, from conquest and genocide to religious wars and devastating plagues. But you're right that there are some big threats facing our whole planet that we can't ignore, as I'll talk about in the Climate & Environment section. There are also a whole lot of people who do care—welcome to our club! (I'm sorry that there's not a cool membership card or anything . . .)

The development of the Internet and social media has made us more aware of the constant suffering going on around the world. After all, for much of human history, people used to be aware only of the bad things happening in their local area, or perhaps they would hear word that something bad had happened elsewhere by word of mouth, or eventually from newspapers. But now we get to see horrible things happening everywhere, often from the convenience of our phones, sometimes even live, and played back to us in seemingly endless loops of pain and trauma. Our bodies weren't designed to be able to withstand that kind of constant anxiety!

As a result, many of us have developed **hypervigilance**, which is when our bodies are constantly on high alert because our nervous systems are waiting for the next bad thing to happen. That's not a sustainable way for us to be able to maintain our health or feel calm and peaceful enough to be able to keep doing good in the world. It is another reason to TAKE BREAKS FROM THE INTERNET! Lol.

Whenever I get overwhelmed by all the horrible things happening in the world, I return again and again to a quote by author Rabbi Rami Shapiro. Rabbi Shapiro offers a modern-day interpretation of a part of an ancient Jewish text called the Mishnah. His translation says: "Do not be daunted by the enormity of the world's grief. Do justly, now. Love mercy, now. Walk humbly, now. You are not obligated to complete the work, but neither are you free to abandon it."

In other words: One person can't change the entire world and solve all its problems. But we all must do what we can to make a difference. Together, we humans have the ability to bring about collective love and justice.

GOVERNMENT

As we get older, we begin to realize that much of the way we live our lives and understand our society is informed by our governments. Our governments dictate our laws, how our tax money is spent, and how our country interacts with other countries around the world. And for the many groups of us who face oppression in one or multiple ways, our government's decisions have a huge impact on our lives.

For example, our governments determine how our country treats immigrants, and thus many members of our families. They decide whether to pass and uphold laws that treat LGBTQQIA2S+ people equally or unfairly. They have the power to give poor families more economic help for food (or not), hold racist police officers accountable (or not), and so much more.

Therefore, it's important to know what's going on in your government. Information, activism, and organizing is how we will create a world with just and compassionate laws and public service officials— and it starts with getting your questions about government answered!

Content note: *This chapter explores at length the mass violence committed by governments against marginalized groups of people, especially people of color (colonization, enslavement, anti-Black laws, the internment of Japanese people, and so on).*

FOR THE PEOPLE, BY THE PEOPLE

QUESTION: Why do governments exist? Do we need them for society to function?

Governments exist to make and enforce laws in a society and establish structures for the good of its citizens. Ideally, governments would make life better for people, though whether this is true differs wildly across the world and within communities in any given country.

Some people think governments are inherently oppressive and violent—those people are called **anarchists**, and they have various ideas for how society could operate without an organized system of laws. There are also **authoritarians**, who believe people should obey the absolute authority of the government. Most people in Western societies fall somewhere in the middle of these two ideas, often preferring some government structure to assist with providing things like electricity, roads and highways, and schools, while also desiring to have a sense of freedom and choice about many aspects of their lives.

A main problem with governments (which is, at its root, a problem with humans!) is that many are made up of people who want to have power over others instead of with others. Put another way, they use their power to exploit others, rather than to protect everyone's rights. Social justice activism aims to push governments to uphold justice for all instead of grabbing power and comfort for some at the expense of others.

> **QUESTION:** What makes a good president or prime minister?

I think that the qualities we should look for in a president or prime minister are generally the same qualities we should look for in any human. This list would, first and foremost, include caring about others and being able to put themselves in the shoes of people who are struggling or facing oppression that they don't personally have to face. They should desire to do what is right so that everyone can have a better life, versus doing what will boost their career or make them money.

A willingness to listen and learn and potentially change their mind about issues once they understand more is also important. They should be able to value people's differences rather than fear them. And they should be okay with taking **accountability**, which means apologizing when they make a mistake and then taking action to do better. They should also care more about having a peaceful world than about proving how their country is better than other countries.

Finally, they should know that we can't have a freer future without uncovering, learning about, and healing the injustices of our nations' histories. Would you add anything to this list? What do you think? After all, you'll be helping to choose your country's presidents or prime ministers in the very near future!

ASK AN EXPERT: Kimberley Latrice Jones is one of my favorite people I've met on the Internet. She writes books and makes films and has super smart ideas about how we can make the political system one that works for all of us. She has the perfect brain for this question.

I love this question! Local, state, and federal (national) governments work together on behalf of the people. Let's start with the largest and work our way down.

The *federal* government makes laws that affect the nation. The federal government oversees the production of currency (money), creates the tax code, sets up social services, and interacts with our international counterparts. It also oversees the military that operates both domestically and abroad. And it provides tools to the state and local governments to be able to manage federally funded programs, such as affordable health insurance, airport construction, maintenance of interstate highways, and environmental protection.

The *state* government controls the state criminal code, maintains state roads, and carries out federal laws and programs within state borders. States are divided into municipalities, which carry out state laws within a specific county or town (i.e., at the *local* level). Towns or cities have mayors and councils to manage public services. Local government responsibilities include managing most public services, like parks, libraries, schools, police, and fire stations.

So as you can see, the federal government, which the president is the boss of, passes down cash and laws to the state, which the governor is the boss of, and it passes down services, laws, and money to the towns, which the mayor is the boss of. It's a massive domino effect of laws, services, and cash that pass down from the federal level. So yes, while local politics are extremely important, it is essential that we realize the huge role national policy plays on a local level.

JUSTICE FOR ALL

QUESTION: Why do my best friend's parents vote for mean politicians who do so many bad things and take away our rights?

I've always wished for a superpower, and if I had one it would be to read minds. It would help me understand a lot of things . . . (But even if I could read minds, it might not help me understand in this case!)

People make political decisions based on a lot of different reasons. They may be influenced by the beliefs they grew up with in their family or community, by churches or other religious establishments, or based on financial and economic experiences. Sometimes they make them based on fear. Fear that they won't have enough and that someone will have something that won't be available to them. (Of course, just like with playground bullies, treating others badly based on your fear is still never acceptable!) Politicians often use that fear to get more votes.

It's important to think about what decisions we would make if we weren't afraid. How do we feel when we're not afraid? Do we feel powerful, strong, clear? Do we feel caring and loving? I imagine that when we feel those things, we might vote for people who reflect how we feel—people who would respect the rights and autonomy of all people.

In addition, far too many people only think about their own interests and what would benefit them when they make voting decisions. For example, someone's parents who are wealthy, heterosexual, and abled (non-disabled) might support a politician who pledges not to tax wealthy people, while ignoring that the candidate they're voting for also supports discriminating against LGBTQQIA2S+ people and taking away money from disabled people. In other words, people can be selfish when they vote.

Someone might support certain policies because they think they won't be harmed by them even if others will. However, often the opposite happens. For example, a white woman who is afraid of immigrants could vote for someone who supports racist policies against immigrant rights. And yet, that same politician may also be against her right to equal pay as a woman or her reproductive rights. (There could also always come a time when she or someone she loves needs to immigrate . . .) Politicians who support oppression in one area usually support the oppression of many marginalized groups. And most humans are or will be part of a marginalized group at some point in their life. This is why it never makes sense to vote for politicians who support oppression.

Of course, people also disagree about what is "good" and "bad" in politics. As I've said, if someone isn't connected to their radical self-love, they may feel like the only way to be "good enough" is to feel like they are better than others. This may encourage them to vote for candidates who believe some groups of people are better than others based on race, ability, culture, or where they come from. These beliefs make it easy to think that harmful policies are "good" policies.

Candidates support this way of thinking by shaping their arguments to appeal to this belief. Rarely will a politician say, "I want to ruin immigrant families' lives by deporting their family members so we can keep our country as white as possible!" Instead, a politician might say, "I'm keeping our borders safe by keeping out criminals!" This is how someone can see themselves as better than immigrants—because their politicians have implied that immigrants are criminals.

When we vote from our radical self-love values, we never need to see ourselves as better or worse than anyone else. This also means we don't have to vote for people who try to make us feel better by telling us other people are worse than us. We all deserve a government and politicians who work to make EVERYONE's lives the best they can be. Supporting candidates who pledge to help people rather than harm them—or running for office yourself someday!—is crucial.

> **QUESTION:** Why are so many people in my country's government against immigrants and refugees?

If you recall, xenophobia is the dislike of people from other countries. Xenophobia is driven by fear and hatred, and it shows up in a whole bunch of sneaky ways.

In Western Europe and North America, **national identity**—people's sense of who they are based on what country they're from—often gets linked to race. Elected officials who are disproportionately white and who are xenophobic often try to pass laws to make their countries as white as possible. In their minds, being an American or a Canadian or a French person (for example) means being white. And they associate being an immigrant or refugee with being a person of color, even though there are white immigrants and refugees. To justify their racism and xenophobia, they make cruel and often inaccurate arguments about why immigrants and refugees don't belong or are even dangerous.

Xenophobic politicians might argue, for example, that Syrian or Afghan refugees will "ruin" French culture and force everyone to become Muslim, or that they're secretly terrorists waiting to attack the countries they're moving to. Or politicians might falsely claim that immigrants and refugees will "take" the jobs of people already living in the country, or that they'll cost taxpayers money because they will participate in government programs designed to help people. These politicians will usually pretend that their home country is in danger of being "taken over" or "destroyed" by immigrants and refugees.

This is an extra sneaky way for white people to ignore the history of how their countries and ancestors have taken over and destroyed other countries. Racism against South Asian immigrants in England, for example, attempts to erase England's long bloody history of colonizing India, while anti-Blackness in France tries to ignore how France invaded and took over more than a dozen African countries!

The vast majority of immigrants and refugees want what everyone wants: safety, happiness, and prosperity for themselves and their families. What anti-immigrant and anti-refugee politicians—as well as the voters who give them their power—refuse to acknowledge is that unless you are an Indigenous person or the descendant of enslaved people, everyone has a history of immigration. Our work is to be gracious to each other as neighbors on this shared planet and members of the human family.

If a person's family members aren't immigrants or refugees, they simply were lucky to be born in an environment they didn't have to flee from. Being born in France doesn't make someone better than or more entitled to a better life than someone from Afghanistan who comes to France for a better life. Remember: In the wrong situation (like war or a natural disaster), any of us could need to become an immigrant or refugee. So how would we want others to treat us? This is the message our governments must hear from us, and politicians who understand this are the ones we want in office.

QUESTION: Why are some countries extremely wealthy while others are poor?

Well, friend, this smart question requires a huge, multi-layered answer. To understand why there's so much inequality around the world, we must, as always, look back at history to see where the story started and how it unfolded over time.

Countries don't become poor or wealthy out of nowhere; greed and theft through violence, colonization, enslavement, and exploitation are always at the root. Europeans colonized many countries and robbed much of the globe of their precious natural resources and their people, creating rich and powerful Western countries while leaving other nations depleted, exploited, and enslaved.

The country of Haiti is a perfect example of this. The island that is now known as the two countries of Haiti and the Dominican Republic was originally called Quisqueya by the Indigenous Taíno people, who populated the island since at least 250 BCE. Quisqueya's economy was driven by farming, fishing, and trading with other islands in the area. This was their way of life for thousands of years.

Then the Italian sailor we know today as Christopher Columbus arrived in 1492. Columbus and other Europeans—namely the Spanish, and then the French—began enslaving the people of Quisqueya, forcing them to mine gold and later other crops like sugar, coffee, and cotton. The Europeans stole the profits of these goods to make their home countries lots of money, all while the people of Quisqueya suffered and died of overwork, starvation, and European diseases. But the Europeans kept bringing in more and more people they had kidnapped in Africa to add to the enslaved populations of what would become Haiti and the Dominican Republic.

Haitians fought back against the French during the 1804 **Haitian Revolution**, becoming the first and only country to gain freedom from enslavement due to a national rebellion. But in 1825, the French sent military boats to Haiti and threatened to attack them if they did not pay France the equivalent of twenty-one BILLION dollars over the next one hundred years to "compensate" the French government for all the money the French lost when they could no longer continue legally enslaving Haitians. Yes, you heard that right: Haiti had to pay France for no longer being enslaved. We could say France were being bullies!

Despite Haiti winning its independence, France kept making money while Haiti sank deeply into debt. Today, Haiti is the poorest country in the Western Hemisphere (the same part of the globe as North and South America) and continues to struggle with corruption and natural disasters. We see how Haiti's history of being robbed of its people and resources has continued to make Europe richer while keeping the Haitian people in poverty.

As if this isn't bad enough, countries in the **Global South**—Africa, Latin America, parts of Oceania, and those parts of Asia and the Middle East most negatively impacted by **global capitalism**—get blamed for their own oppression. What most of these countries have in common is that they are usually low-income and the majority of their populations are people of color. Their poverty is commonly used by people in majority white, wealthy nations as evidence that the poor people of color are inferior to wealthy white people.

This happens WITHIN wealthy Western countries too: Low-income Black and Indigenous people are often stereotyped as "lazy" and "stupid" by white people with racist beliefs, even though there wouldn't be such a big gap in wealth in the first place if European nations hadn't enslaved them, taken over their countries, and passed racist laws to discriminate against them.

As you can see, Western wealth and racism go together like the world's worst peanut butter and jelly sandwich.

MAKING IT MAKE SENSE

QUESTION: When will the COVID-19 pandemic be over?

Although I'm bald, I'm not a crystal ball, and I do not know the future. But I do know that how long COVID-19 continues to take lives and disrupt our social world is dependent on the choices we make as humans.

There are countries, like the one I used to live in (New Zealand), where far fewer people have died of COVID. And most of society can go about its business not being affected by COVID. And that's because, as a nation, people chose to listen to the advice given by scientists and doctors. People chose to be concerned about the safety of their neighbors, wear masks and socially distance or stay at home. And when a vaccine was first available, nearly 90 percent of the country chose to get vaccinated to stay safe and keep others safe.

COVID-19 is a reminder that we are interdependent: Our lives are connected, and we need each other to survive. If we all remember that and act like it's true (because it is), COVID-19 might not entirely go away, but it could cause a lot less harm and death.

This question is so important! The first thing you need to know is that not all sources of information are created equal. If you've ever had to write an essay, your teacher may have told you that you must cite actual books and articles from reputable news organizations in your essay rather than only linking to Wikipedia (which can be a good place to start, but should not be the end of any fact-finding mission, since it doesn't always have the best sources backing up the information shared there). Some good questions to ask when checking to see which information you can trust is: *Who* wrote this, and *how* do they know it? For example, if you wanted to learn more about dinosaurs, would you rather hear from a paleontologist—the type of scientist who studies dinosaurs, who had to go to school for years to learn about dinosaurs before going out and examining actual fossils—or would you rather hear from your uncle Ned, who listened to a random YouTube video with questionable sources and now believes dinosaurs never existed? (Hint: Probably not Uncle Ned!)

A big part of learning how and where to get reliable news and information is to develop your **critical media literacy**. Critical media literacy is the process through which we learn to evaluate different sources of media, comparing how they cover the same issue, what perspectives they highlight, and what they may leave out. The more you're able to compare different sources to each other to see whether it makes sense to trust them or not, the more you'll be able to avoid getting tricked by all that "weird stuff," as you so aptly put it, floating around.

This is crucial for a thriving democratic society. After all, we can't become informed citizens who are educated on issues important to us—much less know which political candidates to vote for, or how to make other positive changes in society—if we don't know how to find the best information out there. You can learn more about media literacy by reading books on it, such as *But I Read It on the Internet!* by Toni Buzzeo.

THE WAY FORWARD

> **QUESTION:** What are some examples of a government doing good things for its people? What things should we look for in a good government?

Just like there are no perfect people, there are no perfect governments. Because governments are made up of humans who make mistakes and can be selfish or greedy—and because most countries have some history of being oppressed or oppressing others—all governments have room to improve. But if we agree that good governments make policies that ensure all their citizens have what they need and are taken care of, then there are some countries doing good things for their people that we can look at.

For example, Namibia, New Zealand, Hong Kong, and nearly two hundred other countries provide universal, free, or extremely low-cost health care to their citizens. Given that all humans will need health care at some point in their life, making sure all citizens can access health-related treatment is part of good governing. Another example of good government policies is free secondary education that better prepares students for higher-paying jobs: Kenya, Panama, and twenty other countries offer free tuition for students attending college. Some of those countries even offer free tuition for international students if you can speak the language.

Another key aspect of a good government is knowing when and how to apologize for the wrongs it has done. In 2021, then prime minister of New Zealand, Jacinda Ardern, participated in an accountability ceremony with Pacific Islanders called a Samoan **Ifoga**. The ceremony was done as part of a formal apology for anti-immigrant policies in the 1970s, called "Dawn Raids," that targeted Pacific Islanders in New Zealand. The raids forcibly removed hundreds of people from their homes and schools who were believed to be illegally living in New Zealand. Most of the people had been invited to the country to work jobs the government could not find employees for. The raids tore apart families and targeted people simply based on their ethnic identity. While some people thought the prime minister should not have apologized, many others felt like her apology on behalf of the government was a necessary step in restoring trust between the government and Pacific Islander communities.

Additionally, governments should not only offer verbal apologies when they've harmed people, but should also include trying to repair the harm and build trust through policies, programs, and **reparations**, which are monetary payments for harm or damage. For example, during World War II, the United States imprisoned over 125,000 Japanese Americans of all ages in internment camps (also known as incarceration camps) from 1942 until 1945. This was both racist and unconstitutional, and caused many Japanese Americans great harm, including severe psychological trauma, loss of property, malnutrition, and the deaths of at least 1,600 people. In 1988, the US government passed the Civil Liberties Act, which gave reparations and a formal presidential apology to the remaining Japanese Americans who survived these camps. Meanwhile in New Zealand in 1995, the government paid some reparations ($170 million in cash and land) to the Indigenous Maori community for stealing their land and a loss of more than half its population as a result of colonization.

Reparations cannot undo the historical violence of a government—for example, in the case of the US, the violence committed against Black people who experienced enslavement and Jim Crow. But reparations can help to reduce some of the economic disadvantages that resulted from the harm.

Ultimately, governments that desire to share power and focus on the well-being of their citizens will create policies that do that and will take responsibility and change when they don't. Unfortunately, there are far too many governments that aren't prioritizing the well-being of their citizens or taking accountability to do better. But I believe that with a generation of young people like you eventually running for office, we can create a government for the people, by the people, that includes ALL people!

QUESTION: Does having a protest actually do anything to change our laws or how people are treated?

It sure does! In fact, many of our most basic rights and freedoms that we have today came from people collectively protesting, risking their lives, and even dying in the attempt to secure them.

Frederick Douglass—a famous abolitionist (someone who fought against slavery)—once said, "Power concedes nothing without a demand." Which was a fancy way to say that too often, governments do not give marginalized people freedom without the people demanding and fighting for it. And that is what brave activists and organizers have done over and over again, forcing the government to change through coming together, organizing, rising up in protest, and using the power of their voices to persuade and inspire.

History is full of successful examples, including plantation uprisings and the abolitionist movement fighting for an end to slavery in the US; the fight for women's suffrage (voting rights) in the US, UK, and Ireland; the US Black civil rights movement leading to the passage of the 1964 Civil Rights Act; the 1968 Stonewall Rebellion in New York City, which signaled the beginning of the modern LGBTQQIA2S+ rights movement; and the labor movement fighting for workers' rights against corrupt bosses, which succeeded in abolishing **child labor**—that is, kids being forced to have jobs, usually in dangerous and unhealthy places like factories or mines. Protests were successful in Western countries in limiting the length of the workday, passing workplace safety laws, and creating the concept of the weekend. And the global protest against the racist South African government brought down apartheid, their system of violent racial segregation. Even small local protests can change laws. In 2023, when the Florida High School Athletic Association wanted to force girl athletes to report the details of their menstrual cycles in order to play school sports, parents and other outraged community members protested until the athletic association withdrew its attempt at forced reporting. Everyday people protest in ways big and small for justice.

As you can see, the list is long and full of people who stood up for their rights, got out into the streets for change, and let their voices be heard. Sometimes those protests give us small victories and sometimes we may not see the results in our lifetime. Nevertheless, having our voices be heard is part of our rights as humans. Governments are supposed to work on behalf of the people—if and when they fail to do so, it's up to us to question and challenge them. What changes will you help make happen in your lifetime?

CLIMATE & ENVIRONMENT

Protecting our environment is central to the protection of all the life that our beautiful planet supports. Without a healthy and balanced **ecosystem**, species—including the human species—cannot survive.

Because many people in power care more about making billions of dollars than they do about protecting life on our planet, they pollute the earth, water, and sky. This results in the climate crisis we are experiencing globally, in which extreme weather has already begun to drastically alter our lives, and animals like polar bears and even bees are threatened.

You probably already know about this since your generation's future is at risk and many of you are engaging in bold and brave activism for climate justice. I'm SO proud of you, and I'm also so sorry that older generations of humans haven't collectively done a better job of taking care of Earth.

Here's the good news: You aren't alone in your efforts. There are many people around the world fighting to protect life on our precious planet. We'll get to hear more about them, and what you can do in your own life to protect our environment, as I try to answer your wise climate questions.

NOT BETTER THAN THE CRITTERS

QUESTION: Why are humans so much more intelligent than other animals (for example, by inventing things and making rules)?

I would offer that I don't know that I agree that humans are more intelligent than other animals. Based on making rules and inventing things, I would say there are other species that do both those things. Take inventing stuff: There's a whole area of scientific invention inspired by nature called **biomimicry**, meaning we get all kinds of things from the genius of animals. For instance, the system of dams? We got that from beavers. And while dams can sometimes flood, we have copied beavers' ingenuity. It's also my hunch that we got the idea of building shelters from seeing animals build shelters (for instance, like birds building nests, or even bears dwelling in dens for the winter).

And if by rules, we mean systems, the natural world has many systems that govern it. There's the root-like system of fungus under trees, for example, called **mycelium,** which spreads underground and help digest and recycle decomposing organisms. There's also the technology of caterpillar DNA, which contains the instructions for the caterpillars to become butterflies from the very beginning of their lives. Animals also have social rules that govern who is in charge in a community, how their young will be cared for, and even how they mate with each other.

So to summarize, I don't think humans are smarter. I think we're all part of an intricate web of intelligence that includes the entirety of the planet and the cosmos. And when we're intentional about it, together we can make a world that allows each of us to reach our highest potential.

> **QUESTION:** Why do humans eat other living beings? I think it's weird and sad but not many people around me agree. Is it possible to have a world where people don't eat other animals?

First, I want to celebrate your kindness and empathy toward non-human animals. You're wise to recognize that there's something special and sacred about all living beings on this planet, and that humans aren't the only animals who deserve respect and care.

To answer your question, people came to eat other animals historically out of survival, like many other species. Animal-based recipes are important to many cultures around the world. But there are some cultures that don't eat certain animals, or who eat very little animal products or even no animal products at all! There are also many Indigenous cultures around the world that eat meat but recognize it as a sacred act, and part of the interdependence of all species. They honor the animals they kill for nourishment and they treat them with respect in the wild, working not to exploit the animals for profit and greed. They seek to be in balance with nature.

Even though you may feel alone compared to the eating habits and preferences of those around you, you're not alone—there are increasing numbers of both **vegetarians** and **vegans** (like me)! Some estimates put the total number of vegetarians and vegans in the world at just over 79 million humans. Vegetarians don't eat meat, while vegans don't eat any products that come from animals, including dairy and honey. People who are vegetarian or vegan for ethical reasons argue that eating animals is an example of **speciesism**, which is the belief that humans matter more than all the other species on our planet. People who refuse to eat animals believe that non-human animals deserve respect and shouldn't be treated as objects for humans to use and abuse. And vegans are particularly concerned about factory farming, specifically dairy farming, which tortures and kills huge volumes of cows and further pollutes the environment for the purpose of making corporations, or big companies, even more profitable.

That said, issues of racism and classism often make it difficult for certain communities to have access to fresh fruits and vegetables or even good grocery stores in their neighborhoods, making vegetarianism and veganism expensive and out of reach for many people. It is also difficult for kids because they often rely on their caregivers or schools to provide what they eat. So depending on where people live, how much money they have, and what their cultural background is, it may or may not be practical to avoid consuming animal products.

But at the end of the day, it's true that curbing how much meat we eat, in addition to improving the lives of non-human animals, will have a positive impact on the environmental crisis. It might help to start small—for example, you might ask your family if you could start doing "Meatless Mondays" and enjoy meals that don't involve animals one day a week. Try it out!

PLANET WORRY

QUESTION: Why am I so worried about climate change when it probably won't even happen in my generation?

My dear, I'm sorry to have to tell you this, but climate change *is* already happening in your generation. It was happening before you were born, even when I was child, but now things are really speeding up: Polar ice caps are melting. Carbon emissions are astronomical. Weather patterns are becoming increasingly extreme, with record heat, cold, wildfires, hurricanes, droughts, and flooding. If we are alive, we are experiencing the impact of climate change. And it'll continue to get worse, especially if we don't take immediate and extreme action.

Climate change can feel scary, and I've felt worried about it as well. For many years I lived in California, and each year, wildfires became more intense and more destructive. Just a couple of weeks before I moved I was driving home from a friend's house and saw a hillside near my home on fire. It was frightening. Luckily, no houses were burned, but every year people lose homes and lives to drought-related fires caused by climate change.

What's also true is that it's not the best use of our energy to worry. As the Vietnamese Buddhist monk and peace activist Thich Nhat Hanh tells us, "Worrying does not accomplish anything. Even if you worry twenty times more, it will not change the situation of the world. In fact, your anxiety will only make things worse. Even though things are not as we would like, we can still be content, knowing we are trying our best and will continue to do so. If we don't know how to breathe, smile, and live every moment of our life deeply, we will never be able to help anyone."

It all comes down to this: If we have energy to worry, we have energy to take action. Action is different from worry because it asks us to do something that will impact our future. I act by being mindful of my water usage and changing how I eat so it has less impact on the environment. I also support climate causes and activists. There are millions of people taking action every day, such as activists who are part of the Sunrise Movement, a grassroots network of young people fighting to take political action for climate justice. We'll talk some more about ways you can help in the following questions and answers.

QUESTION: Why does this generation feel so pressured to change and fix the world?

That's a good question! I don't know why, but I'm so glad you care.

Historically, many of the ways in which the world was organized worked for some people. But those systems—systems of capitalism, colonization, white supremacy, misogyny, and other forms of oppression—were always unsustainable. They require that we pillage resources from the planet, that we harm other people. They require that we be disconnected from our own radical self-love. And none of that can last forever.

The resources that humans extract from the earth and from each other are not everlasting. Eventually, we'll realize that the way we've been doing things doesn't work. Eventually, we'll feel bad for the harm we've caused people. And I believe that your generation can already see how so many of the ways we've tried to organize the world just don't work. They don't work to keep us all safe, to make sure we have what we need, to live healthy and thriving lives. They don't work to help us make a world that benefits everybody. And I, for one, am so grateful that young people can see this so clearly and feel so deeply that it isn't right and has to change.

Every day I am inspired by what young people make possible in the world. And I sure am grateful for you and your generation. However, the responsibility of facing and remedying climate change or any of the world's problems should not fall on the shoulders of young people. Adults and our systems have created much of these crises and we should be working alongside young people to find solutions.

I also think there's a difference between responsibility and pressure. As people alive on this planet, whose lives literally wouldn't be possible without the support of Earth's oxygen, food, or sustainable ecosystems, we all have the responsibility to do our part to be good stewards of this planet. **Stewardship** means you protect and are a guardian of the earth instead of taking and exploiting the resources around you. Stewardship is a way we can practice being in right relationship with ourselves and the earth. Part of why we're here on this planet, I believe, is to live up to the responsibility of being good Earth stewards.

Pressure, on the other hand, is based in fear. It implies that you're not really consenting to this role—that it's being forced onto you. Feeling forced into taking action to protect the earth isn't a very good foundation for a lifelong relationship between us and this beautiful, precious planet. Pressure also can freeze us with fear and keep us from taking any action at all. I think if we all changed how we think about what a just and compassionate relationship to our planet would be, we would realize that taking responsibility for Earth would feel like the natural, joyful thing to do and would be deeply healing. Unfortunately, there are many people who make tons of money by supporting the companies who cause the most pollution and climate damage. We, as people who care about the planet's well-being, can and should use our activism and people power to demand that those companies do better by the planet and us!

> **QUESTION:** Our climate crisis gives me a lot of fear and anxiety. Is there any way that I can help make a difference in the future of the planet and feel less worried about my own future on the planet?

This is a big, necessary question, and it's awesome that you want to help. Thank you for caring about the planet—I'm sure Mother Earth appreciates it! It is essential to care for the planet and environment. When you find yourself getting overwhelmed or worried by the task, I recommend you take some deep breaths, meditate, or go outside in nature and remember how generous and resilient she is, and you are too.

There are so many ways that young people are making a difference when it comes to climate change. You should absolutely lend your brilliance to the fight. You can find groups to join and get involved in the fight for climate justice at www.youngvoicesfortheplanet.com or with the Sunrise Movement, a youth-led movement to stop climate change. Youth climate activists like Mari Copeny ("Little Miss Flint"), Greta Thunberg, Isra Hirsi, Autumn Peltier, Bruno Rodriguez, Xiye Bastida, and Helena Gualinga have all held climate strikes, staged school walkouts, fundraised, and spoke at the **United Nations**, among other activities. There's no reason you can't be one of the voices stepping up for climate care!

I hope you can see that your fears and anxiety about the environment are absolutely warranted, AND that you have the power to be part of the solution. Taking action, no matter how small, all adds up in the fight for our planet's future. And finding community with others committed to environmental justice will help you remember that you're not alone in this quest.

GETTING BACK TO BALANCE

> **QUESTION:** What is a carbon footprint, and should I be doing something about mine? I learned the term environmental justice; what can I do to support it?

A **carbon footprint** describes the amount of carbon dioxide produced in the atmosphere as greenhouse gas emissions due to the actions of an individual person or group of people. In short, it's how much pollution you're responsible for creating as part of living on this planet.

It's important to point out here that corporations, by far, do the most damage. While individual actions are important, businesses and governments are both the biggest polluters and have the most power to fix this issue. And we MUST use organizing and activism to push them to do so. This can include signing climate-related petitions, writing letters to your government officials, or organizing a climate walkout at your school. The organization Voices of Youth has a Climate Action for Youth toolkit for young climate activists to get involved: https://www.voicesofyouth.org/climate-toolkit.

Having said that, in 2017, researchers Seth Wynes and Kimberly A. Nicholas published a paper titled "The Climate Mitigation Gap," which identified the "big four" activities you can change in your daily life that will have the biggest impact on reducing your carbon footprint and interrupting the climate crisis. This "big four" includes having fewer children, living without a car, traveling by air less, and eating a plant-based diet (in other words, not eating meat).

Some people can do these things more easily than others. For example, it's easier not to have a car if you live in a walkable city with plenty of affordable public transit options, but many communities don't have access to reliable public transportation. Without access, it's difficult to survive without a car.

We've also already discussed how plant-based diets may or may not work for people based on what they can afford and what their cultural background is. But these four items are a great place to start, both for you to encourage your parents or caregiver(s) to try out, and for how you live your own life as you become an adult! To learn more about ways to reduce your carbon footprint and help the planet, visit: https://climatekids.nasa.gov/how-to-help/.

QUESTION: Are there any adults actually doing anything to stop the climate crisis? It usually feels like it's only people in my generation who are taking action!

I know it looks like most of us are sleeping on the job, but I promise that there are adults who are passionately engaged in the work of stopping the destruction caused by the climate crisis. I understand why you'd feel like there aren't that many, though: After all, we wouldn't be in this mess in the first place if enough adults had put the well-being of our planet and its species over the selfish desire to make more and more money than they know what to do with.

Indigenous communities all over the world, who have been acting as stewards of the Earth for thousands of years, have been fighting to protect it since the beginning of European colonization. (The idea that the earth is simply here for humans in power to take as many resources and gain as much power over others as they can was a driving force of colonization, after all.) Many Indigenous community members, from elders to youth and everyone in between, have acted as water protectors. These water protectors continue to protest the oil pipelines that capitalists keep building on Indigenous land against the communities' will, and which threaten their access to safe and clean drinking water. Many Indigenous activists are also leading the LANDBACK movement, demanding access to their ancestors' land so they can better manage and protect the earth (such as using traditional wisdom and practices to manage wildfires, for example).

I'm highlighting the role of Indigenous activists because Indigenous communities are often some of the first people to experience the most extreme effects of the climate crisis. This is in large part due to **environmental racism**. Environmental racism refers to the ways in which those in power damage and pollute the environment in low-income communities of color because they consider poor people of color's lives to be less valuable than the lives of wealthy white people.

One example of environmental racism is the town of Flint, Michigan, a mostly Black and working-class city where the water has been poisoned with lead since 2014. Despite years of complaints, the city refused to do anything to solve the problem. Only after national and

GOD & RELIGION

Human beings believe a *lot* of different things about God and religion.

Some of us believe in a higher being or energy we call God, and some of us don't. If we do believe in God, we often have very different ways of understanding exactly what "God" is. Is God male? Female? Non-binary? Is there one god, like Abrahamic religions (Judaism, Christianity, and Islam) believe? Or are there many, as both ancient and modern Hindus and pagans see it? We have a bazillion names for God in all our different languages and cultures around the world, as well as plenty of people who either don't believe in a higher power, or don't believe we can ever know.

There are so many different belief systems that even within one religion, there are many different paths—a few examples include Sunni and Shi'a in Islam; Catholicism, Protestantism, and the Eastern Orthodox Church in Christianity; Orthodox, Conservative, and Reform movements in Judaism; and Theravada, Mahayana, and Vajrayana (Tibetan) Buddhism. Whew!

With all these options—and so many people who claim that they and they alone follow the "right" one—it makes sense that you'd have a lot of questions! Let's examine God and religion more deeply, with no question off-limits.

Content note: *This chapter discusses religious abuse, including sexual abuse, homophobia and transphobia, and religious bigotry by one religion against others. It also discusses anti-Semitism and the mass violence of the Holocaust.*

A BOUNTY OF BELIEFS

QUESTION: Why does religion exist?

Thousands of years ago, humans created spirituality and religion as ways to answer their questions about the world and the universe: Where do we all come from? Where did the cosmos and the earth come from? What is the meaning of life? What should we value as good and what should we see as wrong? How should we treat each other and other animals? And so on. People were looking for guidance in navigating a world that could seem quite confusing at times, and came up with creation stories, religious texts, and various rules to provide just that. For millions of people, religion has helped make sense of life and offer hope. For others, it has been a tool of division, harm, and control. And like most tools, whether it is helpful or harmful depends on how you use it. The world's religions are just as diverse as the humans who made them.

QUESTION: How many religions exist in the world?

The short answer: Too many to name here, and new ones are created probably every day!

The longer answer: There are so many different belief systems all over the world, and so many more that people used to believe thousands of years ago that we only know fragments about today. (Shout-out to the Druids!)

The World Population Review website reports that as of 2020, the biggest religions in the world by number of members are Christianity with 2.38 billion people (31 percent of the world population), Islam with 1.91 billion (24 percent), unaffiliated (which means not belonging to any religion) with 1.2 billion (16 percent), Hinduism with 1.16 billion (15 percent), Buddhism with 507 million (7 percent), **folk religions** (religions practiced by certain ethnic groups, tribes, and cultures in a specific geographic region outside organized religion) with 430 million (6 percent), other religions with 61 million (0.5 percent), Sikhism with 26 million (0.3 percent), and Judaism with 14.6 million people (0.2 percent).

Studying the religions of the world is a great way to learn more about the history of culture, geography, and even language. People with religious studies degrees go on to work in community services, religious centers, and even journalism. Who knows? Perhaps it may be a future path for you.

QUESTION: How do religions explain why bad things happen in the world?

Religions have all sorts of reasons to explain why bad things happen in the world. Some of them include the idea that people are being punished by God for not doing what God wants them to, that evil forces (like Satan) control the world and influence people to do bad things, that the bad things we've done will come back to us as consequence for our behaviors, and that suffering happens as part of life and it's not possible for us as humans to understand why it happens. Some non-religious beliefs about why bad things happen include the fact that people can be influenced by greed and wanting power, as well as the fact that people repeat patterns of traumatic behavior they experienced (like hitting their kids after they were hit as a kid), instead of healing from the pain and trauma. Either way, the answer to why bad things happen is probably one of the most difficult and debated questions humans have ever asked.

When I was in college, my cousin was shot and killed by another young man. At the Baptist church my grandmother attended, the preacher said what happened to my cousin was because of the "devil's" influence on my cousin and the man who killed him. Personally, I'm not sure if I ever believed it was the devil, but I *did* think that my cousin and his killer were acting out of many years of trauma and oppression as young Black men living in impoverished communities.

All of this is to say, I still don't have an answer to why bad things happen, and I think most of us make up stories to explain the difficult parts of life. Sometimes those stories are religious and sometimes not. But I do think if we worked together to end things like oppression and poverty, we might begin to see fewer bad things happening in the world.

QUESTION: What if there isn't a God?

This is a brave question. A lot of people are scared to ask it. I think some folks are afraid that something "bad" like going to hell will happen to them, or that they won't have a purpose in life if there is no God.

For people who have grown up in a certain religion and centered their lives around a specific understanding of God, the idea that there might not be one can turn their whole world upside down. The truth is, no one knows with complete certainty whether and how God exists. People who don't know if God exists, or who believe it's impossible for humans to know the answer, are called **agnostics**. And people who believe God doesn't exist or that there's no proof for God's existence are called **atheists**. Plenty of people find meaning in life whether they believe in a higher power or not.

There are also so many different ways that people around the world understand the idea of "God" and so many ways to refer to a higher cosmic source: God, Goddess, Great Spirit, Allah, Elohim, Adonai, and specific deities (another word for gods, goddesses, and higher powers) like Vishnu, Shakti, Shiva, Gaia, Pan, Hecate, Oshun, Egun, and so very many more! So when we ask if "God" exists, which one are we talking about? A certain god(dess) from the list above? The idea of them overall? What is our definition of "God"?

Ultimately, whether or not God (as any specific religion or spiritual path imagines him/her/them) exists, I offer that what's most important in this life is that our beliefs direct us to be kind, compassionate people who value love and seek justice for all people. Hundreds of millions of people across this globe are making a difference in each other's lives every day, and they come from every religious background and no religious background at all! Whatever made the bees and trees and oceans has got to be a fan of that!

Churches, temples, and mosques, headed by religious leaders with specific texts and rules about what their members should and shouldn't do, are often referred to as "**organized religion.**" For many people, especially those who grew up in a religion that ultimately wasn't the right fit for them, traditional religious institutions have been discriminatory, unfair, or unethical. A person's experience with the Catholic Church, for example, may become confusing and traumatizing if they believe in many Catholic teachings but are sexually abused by a priest and their church covers it up. Or a person who is gay may realize it no longer makes sense or feels right to attend their church if it's teaching that gay people are sinful and need to change.

When people talk about spirituality, on the other hand, they usually mean something less focused on specific religious rules or requirements. **Spirituality** is a broad term that typically involves a belief in a higher power, deity, or deities, and/or reverence for the universe, but in a way that allows people to choose for themselves what beliefs and practices make the most sense to them. It could involve believing in some things from one religion and other things from another religion. It could also mean not identifying with one religion but keeping certain beliefs, such as reincarnation (the idea that people's souls live many different lifetimes), or worshiping the power of nature.

Ultimately, when a person says they're spiritual and not religious, it often means they still have beliefs about the universe and our place in it—just not in a way that corresponds with what an organized religion expects of its members.

223

FINDING YOUR PATH

> **QUESTION:** Is it okay to question what society/my parents have taught me about religion and God?

You should know by now that I believe it is okay to question anything! Questioning religion as we get older is normal and very common. And it's always important to question our values as we grow older in order to make sure that our beliefs and actions are coming from an authentic place inside us, rather than because someone told us to think that way.

Of course, it can still feel like a super sensitive subject. After all, our families (or society) may often feel very strongly that we should believe what they believe, and that their views about religion or God are the "right" ones. Some may fear that if we don't believe what they believe, we will be bad people, suffer pain and hurt, or even go to hell. This can put tons of pressure on us to just agree with the beliefs that we've always been taught.

But religious beliefs and beliefs about God are an extremely personal experience. Life is about learning to listen to our own intuition, hearts, and minds and finding the path that feels the most authentic for us. This journey of belief is why people often convert from one religion to another, and why over a billion people do not follow any specific religion at all.

Take some time to learn about different religions or philosophies if that's something that interests you. Think of it this way: Even if you decide you want to continue practicing the same religion as your family or most of your society, by studying you'll know more about other religious pathways and have an opportunity to compare it to what you were taught by your parents or society. You can make an informed decision!

Questioning why society or your family believes certain things and acts in certain ways makes you a critical thinker, and critical thinkers make the world better. (Think about it: Without critical thinking, people run the risk of believing and doing whatever they're told, which allows for dangerous things like human rights violations, oppressive governments, and wars!) Plus, in the process, you'll have learned more about the fascinating ways people find meaning as they move through this world, and that's a huge win in my book.

> **QUESTION:** What are some "red flags" (warning signs) I should pay attention to when it comes to deciding what religion, if any, to be? What makes a religion right or wrong for me?

This is such a thoughtful question. If everyone asked this question, learned about red flags, and listened carefully to their intuition, the world would be much better off! We should always be aware of red flags with the people and belief systems we're engaging with, both to better protect ourselves and others. Of course, I cannot tell you what will make a religion right or wrong for you. That's too much responsibility for little old me! But if you decide you want to be a part of a certain religion, it should be because YOU want to, not because anyone else is making you feel guilty or pressured.

Your **faith** should bring you joy and make you feel connected to the universe in a way that improves your life. And it shouldn't make you feel like you're bad, need to change something core about your identity (like your sexual orientation or gender), or tell you to stop listening to your own intuition.

Religion, sadly, has a long history of being used to treat various groups of people badly, such as the use of Christianity to justify colonization, mass murder, and the destruction of people's cultures and Indigenous religions all over the globe. Any group that condones treating people badly is probably bad news.

You should always remember that your radical self-love can help to steer you toward what feels right in your heart. It should be a guiding star that you trust more than what anyone else, even a religious leader, says.

Groups that try to separate you from people you love, or make you harm yourself or others, are groups to stay away from. They may be **cults**, which are small religious groups that are not part of a larger and more accepted religion, and that have beliefs regarded by many people as extreme or dangerous. Cults are often run by one charismatic, popular leader who holds most of the power. Cults often ask members to isolate themselves from their families and friends, and may ask them to give all their money or resources to the cult. Most cults don't allow you to question what the leader says and may use shame, verbal abuse, and/or physical abuse to maintain control.

A group using any of these tactics should be a giant red flag to get OUT, similar to red flags in any other type of abusive relationship.

Likewise, any religion that looks down on other religions, says their religion is better than other religions, or tries to make it seem okay to treat some people better than others (like men over women, or white people over Black and brown people, or heterosexual people over queer people) is probably not rooted in love. At the end of the day, why would you even want to follow something that isn't interested in love?

QUESTION: My religion teaches that homosexuality is wrong, and even though I try not to believe it, it's like that teaching is stuck way, way down inside me, so much that I think maybe it's true.

ASK AN EXPERT: Minister Blyth Barnow is a queer Christian preacher and community organizer who is all about supporting and uplifting groups of people who are often treated poorly and left out of Christian communities. She does this work through Femminary, her queer femme approach to Christianity. She is a friend and an incredible spiritual leader! I just knew that Minister Blyth would be the perfect person to talk about queerness and religion in a way that is loving and empowering for any queer kids reading this book.

Some people talk about God as the still, small voice deep within us, the part of us that just "knows." But sometimes other voices or feelings can get in the way of hearing that voice clearly. If you've been part of a faith community that teaches it's wrong to be gay, it makes sense that some of those messages and voices may linger around for a while.

Those messages are rooted in complex and harmful systems like homophobia, transphobia, white supremacy, and colonization. Those systems are widespread and sticky, so it takes time to sort through their voices in order to hear our own. Be patient with yourself. Stay curious. Notice feelings that come up and spend some time with them. Uncertainty is okay. Being in the process of learning new things or letting go of things you thought were true is nothing to be ashamed of.

Growing up, I went to a church that told me it was wrong to be queer. Yet there was something in me that knew that wasn't true. My still, small voice knew the church was wrong, but I also worried they were right. I was afraid I didn't belong, that there was something wrong with me.

I found it helpful to notice my feelings, to listen to the contradictory voices, to hear and feel them out before making up my mind. When we can pay deep attention to our feelings and all the messages in our minds, it makes it easier to find what we honestly believe.

Work toward turning the volume up on your still, small voice over the voices of others. It might help to write, draw, or go for walks in nature and just listen. Get quiet with yourself, so you can hear yourself. It took time, but I now know that my church is not God. God is God. And homophobia can never be holy.

By taking time to honestly listen to my feelings and get clear on where they came from, I'm able to feel powerful and sure of my beliefs. I knew I landed somewhere true when my own still, small voice was calm, sure, and free of fear. Now it feels like when I trust my gut, I am trusting God within me. And I know that God loves me just as I am.

QUESTION: My friend told me their family said they can't hang out with me anymore because my family isn't the same religion as theirs. Why does this matter, and did I do something wrong?

No, my friend, you didn't do anything wrong. We should all be free to practice whatever religion feels right for us, or no religion at all.

It's okay that we're all different, but some people's families don't agree with that and think kids should only be friends with other kids who are like them. In some religions, kids are taught that only people from their religion are good and trustworthy people. But as I've said many times in this book, "different" doesn't mean "bad" or "wrong."

Excluding people doesn't happen only in a religious context—it happens every time a white family tells their kids they can't hang out with a Black friend in their neighborhood, every time a wealthy family doesn't want their kids to play with kids from families with less money, and every time a homophobic caregiver stops their kid from having a sleepover at a home with queer parents. But we're not wrong for existing unapologetically in our differences—what's wrong is judging people as being "less than" without taking the time to get to know them.

In a perfect world, your friend's family would welcome you, no matter your religion. This concept is called **religious pluralism**. Religious pluralism means a basic respect for other religions so that people from different religious backgrounds can live together peacefully in society. And maybe, had you been allowed over, you all could have had an **interfaith dialogue**. This is when people from different religious backgrounds come together to get to know each other better, learn about each other's religious and spiritual traditions, and gain a better appreciation for both the diversity of everyone's differences and the values they share, like loving one another.

But instead of an interfaith discussion, your friend's family made judgments before getting to know you, and I'm so sorry about that. I hope you're able to see that it's your friend's family who have some growing to do here. You, however, seem open-minded and wise, and I know, with time, you'll make friends who reflect those awesome qualities back at you.

I know you can't see me, but imagine me giving you a big old round of applause for this incredibly brave question. Your choice to examine your family's beliefs and be honest with yourself about how they do not feel supportive of the issues and communities that matter to you is evidence of great maturity. And your interest in exploring religions and beliefs that better align with your values is not only an act of radical self-love, but it also shows the kind of critical thinking skills that will help you tremendously in life.

And yes, there are many examples of religious views that embrace women's and LGBTQQIA2S+ equality! You'll find these views among Unitarian Universalists, reform Jews, progressive Muslims, and most neopagans, for just a few examples. Within these traditions are LGBTQQIA2S+ religious leaders; female and feminist rabbis, cantors, priests, pastors, high priestesses, high priests, and imams; and movements to expand LGBTQQIA2S+ rights and gender equality.

If you desire an inclusive faith community, I promise there is one out there for you. This is a place where an Internet search is your friend. Remember, you can always access your own spiritual guidance by learning to listen to your inner voice about what feels right and what doesn't. You can take the parts of religion that align with you and help you live your most authentic and compassionate life.

A FOUNDATION OF FAITH

QUESTION: I know that a person's religion can help them through some hard times. What are some examples of religion being comforting and hopeful for people who are hurting?

It's true: For many people, religion and spirituality are important tools they rely on for strength, hope, and community during times of distress. I used to tell my atheist friend, "It is a privilege to have never needed a God." What I meant was that for groups who have faced systemic oppression, it's often our religious beliefs, practices, and faith in God that helped us survive unthinkable pain and suffering.

For example, when white colonists forcibly abducted African communities and brought them to the Caribbean islands and the Americas as enslaved people, these African and Afro-Caribbean populations held on to many of their religious practices from across West and Central Africa, even as they were forced to convert to Christianity. Despite being kidnapped and transported across the Atlantic Ocean and forced to abandon their languages, they still found a way to combine their ancestral religions with this new religion of Christianity and create a faith practice of their very own.

Over time, some of these beliefs and practices became known as Hoodoo. These practices were used to pray, communicate with ancestors and spirits, promote healing from illness, and seek protection from—and sometimes escape—the violence of slavery. There are still people who practice Hoodoo today; they're called rootworkers or conjure men and women.

Additionally, the creation of Black churches after the end of the US Civil War provided important spaces for Black Americans to gather in community and organize to continue fighting for their human rights. Over time, Black churches became one of the most important institutions for Black people's activism during the Civil Rights movement.

Another example of religion helping marginalized people through hard times is Jewish people holding on to their religion even during the most horrifying years of the Holocaust. During World War II, German dictator Adolf Hitler led a far-right movement called the Nazi party and instructed Nazi soldiers to torture and murder primarily Jewish people, with the additional targeting of LGBTQQIA2S+ people, disabled people, people of color, and anyone who spoke out against the Nazis. During this time, referred to as the Holocaust, the Nazis and their allies killed around six million Jews.

And yet, so many Jewish people continued to practice Judaism in spite of this persecution. There is a famous photograph of a lit menorah (a candle holder used in Judaism) in a family's window during Hanukkah in 1932 in Kiel, Germany. The menorah, owned by Rabbi Dr. Akiva Posner and his wife, Rachel, can be seen in the window across the street from a large building flying a Nazi flag. This photo captures an incredibly brave act of defiance, in which the Posners chose to keep practicing their faith despite danger and potential death. It serves as a reminder of the long history of Jewish communities using their faith to survive for thousands of years through all kinds of hardship and violent oppression. (The Posner family was thankfully able to escape Germany the following year when Hitler officially became the leader of Germany—a powerful example of folks who were defiant and SURVIVED to tell about it.)

All that said, though, it's important to remember that religion is just one way among many that people find comfort and hope for survival. Faith means trusting that there's something good out there in the universe for us despite what we're going through right now. And that trust can come from believing that God, our ancestors, or other powerful forces in the universe are watching out for us. It can also come from believing in something like the power of people who care about each other, and who are dedicated to creating a better future for everyone.

Regardless of what you believe in that helps you during a hard time, what matters is the love and hope that shine through it.

QUESTION: If religion didn't exist, would people stop fighting with each other over their differences and be able to live in peace?

Don't I wish. Unfortunately, humans have used non-religious reasons to fight and oppress others throughout history. Like scientists in the nineteenth century using the theory of **eugenics** to pretend white people were better than people of color, for example, or atheist dictators using their power to hurt many groups of people.

Religion did not create oppression, even if it was—and is—often used to further it. Oppression comes from people wanting power over others because they are disconnected from their power within— their own radical self-love, the type of love that lets you love others just as much.

In other words, religion can be used as a tool to justify violence and discrimination, but oppression is much bigger than religion. Just as religious people aren't automatically better or more moral than non-religious people, non-religious societies aren't automatically filled with love and peace. Humans committed to pursuing love, justice, and peace are what create societies filled with love, justice, and peace, regardless of their religious beliefs.

CLOSING

Well, my brain, heart, and spirit feel thirty times bigger after spending time with all of these awesome, wise, wild, and necessary questions! My dear readers, I hope you've found some answers to questions you've been thinking about, as well as answers to questions you didn't even think to ask. I hope your brain, heart, and spirit feel bigger after having read this book.

You are not alone in trying to figure out what life is all about—none of us have all the answers, and that is A-OK. Life is about taking the journey, choosing the winding path, and seeing where it all leads. If you trust your heart and remember that you came to this planet already enough, just as you are, you'll find your way.

In other words, if you follow your own radical self-love, you'll do all right. Of course, I can't promise things will never be difficult, but I can promise that, through radical self-love, you'll be adding your unique and oh-so-important gifts to creating a world built on justice and love. Personally, I think that rocks.

If you still have questions that were *not* answered here (pssst . . . of course you will), I hope you will find a loving and trustworthy adult to ask. I hope you find one hundred loving and trustworthy adults. Bravely look for them—they are out there, and I promise they want to help you. You might also share this book with other young people. Together I bet you can come up with even more questions to explore together in community! Remember: Change only happens when we're willing to ask the hard questions . . . and seek out radical answers.

Life is not a solo project. You need support, friends, family, community, society, and more. You need other people, and other people need you. We need each other. You have something spectacular to offer the world, friend. And I can't wait to see it. But by now, I'm sure you already know that.

With radical love,
Sonya

10 TOOLS FOR RADICAL SELF-LOVE

1. DUMP THE JUNK.

What we watch, listen to, and share can add to the oppression of our own and other people's bodies by making us feel like our bodies are bad, wrong, invisible, dehumanized, shameful, or a joke.

What Can You Do?

Remove yourself from all media for twelve hours. (*Yikes! Seriously??*) YES! I know it sounds like forever, but give yourself a twelve-hour media break today and I promise you'll feel better. Instead of consuming media during those hours, you might go outside and enjoy nature, start an art project, write in your journal, hang out with a friend or family member, play with your pet, or any number of other fun things. Try to schedule your break during the time you might usually be on social media. And by "social media," I'm also including the Internet, TV, and print media like newspapers and magazines.

Try some radical reflection. Pay attention to the daily amount of media you take in (social media, music, TV, movies, podcasts, billboards, flyers, YouTube, etc.). As you watch, listen, or scroll today, count the number of negative body messages you come across.

Notice those that feel directed at your body. Notice those that feel directed at others' bodies. While you notice these things, try not to get overwhelmed by shame—instead, work on noticing without judgment. By this I mean, pay attention to the messages you get and how they make you feel, but try not to tell yourself that how you're feeling is "good" or "bad," or that you "should" be feeling some other way. We can radically reflect without judging or shaming ourselves.

2. CURB BODY BAD-MOUTHING.

When we discuss our bodies, personalities, and identities in a negative way, not only do we get further away from our own radical self-love, but people within earshot will compare themselves too. By that I mean others might start wondering whether they should feel ashamed about themselves when they hear you judging those same traits in yourself. They might even worry you could judge them as harshly as you're judging yourself. Our shame harms the radical self-love of others.

What Can You Do?

No body bad-mouthing! Notice the times you start to say something critical about yourself and your body. Each time you catch yourself, stop and give yourself a compliment. You can also give someone else around you a compliment. Try to share compliments that acknowledge *personality, character, skill,* and *talent* rather than physical traits. Notice the reactions of the people you give compliments to. Did you make someone smile? If so, awesome!

Write compliments on Post-it Notes and stick them to your mirror, your friend's locker, or a teacher's desk. It's a great way to spread a bit of radical self-love.

3. REFRAME YOUR FRAMEWORK.

Your body is NOT the enemy. If a coat doesn't fit, it's no one's fault; it just doesn't fit!

What Can You Do?

Don't think of your body as the enemy, but as a teammate, working for what is best for YOU! Ask yourself, "If I think of my body as my teammate, doing its very best for me, how would I go about doing _____?"

4. MEDITATE ON A NEW AFFIRMATION.

An affirmation, as I've discussed earlier in this book, is a positive statement you say to yourself to build your radical self-love. Affirmations usually counter something negative you believe about yourself. For example, an affirmation could be "I deserve to be treated as nicely as I treat my friends and family." Affirmations help you connect to what you need right now, let go of the past, and get your head out of obsessing about what might happen in the future. Get in the now.

What Can You Do?

Are you worried about the future? Are you judging your past actions? None of those things are in the "right now."

Focus on right now. Think of a mantra that will help you remember that you are a spectacular human. Something like "I am connected to my greatness and brilliance." Every time you find yourself living in the past, or worrying about the future, take a deep breath and say your mantra out loud, or in your head. Say it several times a day to help bring you into the present moment.

5. BANISH THE BINARY.

Banish "either/or" ways of thinking. Binary thinking, also sometimes called black-and-white thinking, is when we assume that there are only two ways of thinking about something, and we get frustrated that we can't find a solution. But often when we think *beyond* those two options, we can see that there are more ways of looking at a problem or situation, and we can let our brain be creative and help us figure out what to do!

What Can You Do?

Notice when you use binary and extreme language, like saying "I ALWAYS mess up," or "I NEVER know the right answer." Another example is saying things like, "GIRLS do THIS and BOYS do THAT." When you catch yourself using binary language, think of a different way to phrase it. Instead of saying "I mess up everything!" try "Sometimes, I make mistakes."

6. EXPLORE YOUR TERRAIN.

Knowing our bodies helps us better care for our bodies. Being disconnected from our bodies is often how we miss early signs that we're getting sick or have other health issues. When we're intimately familiar with our own bodies, we can advocate for our health, our safety, and our pleasure.

What Can You Do?

Get to know your own body when it's healthy so you notice when something isn't normal for YOU. Try this: Find a mirror, and really look at different parts of your body. Draw different parts of your body, and remember that our bodies change with time. Find a health care provider you trust to answer your questions honestly and in a non-biased manner at every stage of your development.

7. BE IN MOVEMENT.

Stop moving in ways that don't feel good. If movement doesn't feel loving, it isn't radical self-love! Move in ways that bring you joy!

What Can You Do?

Remember the things you loved to do when you were younger, and that maybe you still like to do: dancing, running, cartwheels, spinning in circles, Hula-Hooping, playing in the water, rolling down a hill, sledding, swaying to music, playing hopscotch, and so many other things! Commit to doing at least two of those things in the next week.

8. MAKE A NEW STORY.

Most shame is attached to a story. We can choose which story we want to live in.

What Can You Do?

One of the best things about reading fairy tales is the complete power of imagination. We can imagine ourselves in the story as a princess, a powerful wizard, or a talking dog. In stories, there are no boundaries for our possibilities. Can you remember that feeling?

Making a new story returns us to that experience of having endless possibilities. Allow yourself the magic of a radical self-love possibility with NO boundaries! Make up a new story. No, really write out a story about a time you felt ashamed, but now tell it from the perspective of feeling totally powerful. How would it change your actions? How might it change the outcome of the story? Try it and see if you feel more empowered after reading this new and improved version! Remember: You can always create a new story without shame and judgment.

9. BE IN COMMUNITY.

Community is one of the most important resources we will have in our lives. Finding people who understand us allows us to face the bigger challenges of growing up. Super smart researcher and friend of mine Dr. Brené Brown says, "If we can share our story with someone who responds with empathy and understanding, shame cannot survive." I absolutely believe her.

What Can You Do?

Talk about important issues with a caring friend group. Consider joining a community that supports you. Check out the Resources section in the back of the book for ideas!

10. GIVE YOURSELF SOME GRACE.
THIS IS THE MOST IMPORTANT TOOL.

Historic systems of power and control—the systems that created the hateful "-isms" and "-phobias" like racism, sexism, fatphobia, homophobia, transphobia, and ableism—want you to feel isolated and ashamed so they can make money off products that supposedly fix your "problems." While we try to avoid these systems that are so deeply ingrained in our society, it's okay to have days when we don't like our bodies. I call these BRB days (Body Road Bump days). Remember that it is possible to love your body (and your whole self!), even when you don't always like it.

COMMUNITY CONVERSATION AGREEMENTS

(Developed from The Body Is Not an Apology's Community Agreements)

CREATE SHAME-FREE CONVERSATIONS.

Any comments that make someone feel bad or ashamed of their body, whether based on race, age, size, gender, disability, sexual orientation, religion, mental health, or anything else, are not okay. This is not how we show love and care for each other, and it doesn't allow us to build trust with each other.

BE CURIOUS AND RESPECTFUL INSTEAD OF DEBATING AND ARGUING.

Sharing and listening to each other's perspectives is so important. This is how we learn and better understand each other instead of just getting angry.

WELCOME THE OPPORTUNITY TO THINK ABOUT MULTIPLE PERSPECTIVES.

We aren't always right. Sometimes we're wrong, and it's okay to admit that. That's how we learn! The more perspectives we listen to, the more we can figure out what we believe and why. Also, if we feel like the person we're talking to is just judging us, we often won't want to take the time to really open up and share what we think and feel. Let's make room for the fact that none of us know everything!

COMPASSION IS KEY.

When we have conversations with each other, we need to remember that we don't all know the same things. We haven't all read the same books or gone to the same schools or had the same teachers or life experiences. When we remember this and take the time to care about how our different lives have given us diverse types of knowledge and insights, that makes us more patient with each other.

IT'S NORMAL TO FEEL UNCOMFORTABLE WHEN LEARNING ABOUT HOW PEOPLE EXPERIENCE DISCRIMINATION AND OPPRESSION, ESPECIALLY WHEN YOU'VE NEVER HAD TO THINK ABOUT IT BEFORE.

We are all exposed to racism, sexism, classism, homophobia, transphobia, xenophobia, ableism and other forms of oppression in our society because we live in an oppressive society. None of us can escape that. You might feel lots of negative emotions when you're learning about things you've never been through, like if you're a white person learning about the reality of anti-Black racism, or a heterosexual person learning about what queer people go through in a homophobic society. You might not want to deal with those emotions because they feel too overwhelming. You might feel guilty that you're treated better than some people in society based simply on how you were born. You might even wonder if it's really *that* bad, because you haven't had to go through it yourself. (News flash: It really *is* that bad!) And you will likely feel sad, scared, angry, or all of the above that people you love and care about are being discriminated against.

Thinking about all this, it makes sense that you'd feel uncomfortable. This is new, unfamiliar, and upsetting information to learn. But being uncomfortable doesn't mean you should turn away and stop trying to help make things better. If we're willing to get uncomfortable, that's how we can change the world together. And that is oh so worth the discomfort.

It's good to remember that often, people who care about us say things to us that aren't meant to make us feel bad. At the same time, though, we all must care about both the *intent* and the *impact* of what we say to people. The *intent* is the thing we're trying to express, even if our message isn't understood by others. The *impact* is the way you make someone feel by what you said, even if that's not what you meant.

For example, if you told your friend, "Whoa! You got an A on that test!" your intent might be to compliment them. Your intent could be good, and that's important. But if you sound extra surprised when you say that sentence, your friend might feel like you think they're usually not smart enough to do well on tests. In which case, the impact of what you just said is negative.

To summarize: It's important to think about *what* we say and *how* we say it when we communicate. Let's give each other space to speak, and also, let's listen to how our words land for others, pause to reflect, and make extra space for taking accountability for our actions if they end up being harmful.

TAKING CARE OF OURSELVES IS IMPORTANT!

Sometimes talking about upsetting things can be . . . well . . . upsetting! It's important to take breaks to support our mental health and come back to hard conversations when we feel more calm and less scared or angry. This will help us give each other the compassion, respect, and patience that we all deserve when we have conversations.

If you're getting upset about something and need to take a break, it's always a good idea to create a boundary by saying, "I care about our conversation, and I need some time to think about it. Let's talk about this more tomorrow (or another specific time)."

CHANGING THE SUBJECT ISN'T HELPFUL WHEN SOMEONE IS TRYING TO LET YOU KNOW HOW YOU HURT THEM.

Sometimes when people feel uncomfortable talking about hard topics, they try to avoid dealing with it by changing the subject. This can happen a lot when someone does something that hurts someone else, and then they don't want to deal with admitting they caused pain or take accountability to do better. Changing the subject instead of taking accountability is called **derailing.** Derailing isn't a fair thing to do to each other, and it prevents us from having meaningful and caring conversations.

NO BULLYING!

Calling people names, being sarcastic, and doing other mean things are the opposite of having a good conversation. Our dialogue breaks down when we hurt each other. Why bother trying to connect with each other if we're just going to cause pain?

ASKING QUESTIONS, INCLUDING ABOUT OURSELVES, IS ENCOURAGED.

As we say on The Body Is Not an Apology's website: "Part of helping people sort through their own ideas and beliefs is to ask questions about those ideas. That includes asking OURSELVES hard questions: *Why do I believe this? What am I afraid of? What am I gaining or losing by trying on a new perspective?* The answers that we are most likely to remember and practice are the ones we come up with ourselves. Dialogue and exchange of ideas help us come up with our own answers."

WHEN YOU DON'T KNOW WHAT SOMEONE MEANT, IT'S BEST TO ASK THEM.

We can go through a lot of hurt when we react to someone based on what we think they meant versus directly asking them what they meant. Sometimes we might think someone was trying to be mean to us when they were actually trying to do the opposite!

BELIEVE IN PEOPLE'S EXPERIENCES.

A big part of having respect for each other is really listening and believing that the experiences of the people you love and care about are real, even if it's not something you've experienced. For example, if you're a cisgender boy, you haven't personally experienced sexism. Believe your sisters and female friends, cousins, neighbors, and other girls and women around you when they tell you how they experience it. It's not right when we dismiss each other, call each other liars, or tell people in our lives that we think they're making up their experiences. Let's stay curious and learn more from one another, instead of making each other feel unsafe and unheard.

CELEBRATE OUR DIFFERENCES.

Celebrating our differences means embracing how we can all be our realest, boldest, sparkliest, most AMAZING selves without being scared or ashamed. We can identify and respect the differences that exist among us, and we can also consider when some differences aren't around us and ask why. For example, if we notice that there aren't many disabled kids at the park, could it be because the sidewalks weren't built to care about people's wheelchairs and other mobility aids? How could our town or city change that?

When we honor and celebrate all our differences, we welcome EVERYBODY and EVERY BODY!

THE GOAL OF COMMUNICATING WITH EACH OTHER IS RADICAL, UNAPOLOGETIC LOVE!

Love is the most important thing about life on this planet. There's nothing higher to aim for than love. This whole book, and our discussions in it, all our tackling of the problems and worries and forms of discrimination we encounter, as well as finding ways to make life better for everyone—it all comes from a place of love.

Whenever you don't know how else to talk to people, start there. Aim your compass at the North Star of love—including, first and always, radical self-love—and there you'll find your destination.

GLOSSARY

Ableism: Discrimination against disabled people.

Accommodations: For disabled people, changing something about a task or the environment you're in so that what you're able to do matches up with what you're trying to get done. For example, an accommodation for a blind student could be making sure books at the library are available in braille, or an accommodation for a student with a learning disability could be giving that student more time to finish their test.

Accountability: Apologizing when you make a mistake, then taking action to do better.

Activism (social justice): Advocating for justice, freedom, and equality for groups of people who are being discriminated against in society. Activism can take on many forms, from protests, strikes (refusing to work for an unfair boss until employees are treated better), and boycotts to raising awareness through educational and fundraising campaigns. Activists (those who engage in activism) are responsible for the major gains marginalized groups have made and continue to make in society.

ADHD (Attention-deficit/hyperactivity disorder): A common condition where people find it hard to concentrate and often act before thinking. Can be helped with therapy and/or medication.

Adultism: When adults think they know everything, and that kids know less because they're younger. A form of ageism.

Affirmations: Positive, kind statements we can make about ourselves to help build our radical self-love.

Ageism: The devaluing of—and discrimination against—people based on their age.

Agender: Not identifying with any gender, or not experiencing yourself as having a gender.

Agnostics: People who don't know if a higher power exists, or who believe it's impossible for humans to know.

Allosexual: Someone who experiences sexual attraction to others.

Amatonormativity: The assumption that everyone will eventually develop romantic relationships and become one-half of a couple.

Anarchists: People who think governments are inherently oppressive and violent. Anarchists have various ideas for how society could operate without an organized system of laws.

Anti-Semitism: Hatred and discrimination against Jewish people.

Anxiety: A mental health condition caused by stress and trauma, in which you often feel anxious, worried, and nervous, to the point where it interferes with daily life. Anxiety is typically the result of your body trying to keep you safe by alerting you to all the possible dangers—real or imagined—around you.

Apartheid: A racist set of policies meaning "apart-ness," enacted by the South African government from the mid- to late twentieth century, in which every aspect of society became racially segregated and white people were treated better than people of color through "white laws." Apartheid was dismantled in the 1990s after decades of protests in South Africa and globally.

Aromantic ("aro"): Someone who experiences little to no romantic attraction.

Asexual ("ace"): Someone who experiences little to no sexual attraction.

Atheists: People who don't believe in a higher power or think that there's no proof of a supreme being.

Authoritarians: Those who believe people should obey the abso-lute authority of the government.

Binary: A strict set of two opposite options. For example, the gender binary is the assumption that there are only two types of genders, male and female.

Biology: The branch of science that studies living things, including humans, non-human animals, plants, trees, and every other living thing in our world.

Biomimicry: Scientific inventions inspired by nature. For example, human-made dams that resemble the structure of beaver dams.

Bisexual: Someone who is sexually and/or romantically attracted to two or more genders.

BMI (Body Mass Index): A flawed method of determining what the "average" human should look like; invented by nineteenth-century social scientist Adolphe Quetelet.

Body shame: The outcome of internalizing negative messages from the outside world about our bodies, which chips away at our radical self-love.

Body Shame Profit Complex: A term created by Sonya Renee Taylor to describe the global system through which beauty companies make people feel bad about their bodies in order to make billions of dollars off products that will "fix" these "flaws."

Boundaries: The physical and emotional guidelines for behavior that you will and won't accept from others.

Boycott: When people protest corrupt companies by refusing to buy their products and spreading the word to others until the companies agree to change their behavior.

Capitalism (Global): An economic and political system in which trade and industry are controlled by private owners for profit. "Global capitalism" refers to this practice around the world.

Carbon footprint: The amount of carbon dioxide produced in the atmosphere as greenhouse gas emissions due to the actions of an individual person or group of people; how much pollution you're responsible for creating as part of living on this planet.

Child labor: Children being forced to work, usually in dangerous and unhealthy places like factories or mines.

Cisgender: Someone who continues to identify with the gender they were assigned at birth.

Classism: Discrimination based on someone's social or economic class, specifically someone who is poor or working-class.

Climate migrants: People forced to flee their home countries or regions because climate change has made their homes unlivable.

Colonization: When one nation takes over and exerts control over another nation, violently erasing much of their history and culture.

Colorblindness: When talking about race, it's the misguided idea that we can end racism by ignoring each other's differences and pretending they don't exist.

Colorism: Valuing lighter skin more than darker skin, even among people of color; a tool of white supremacist delusion.

Coming out: When someone informs others that they're part of the LGBTQQIA2S+ community, because we live in a heteronormative (see "heteronormativity") society that often assumes heterosexuality (see "heterosexual").

Consent: The act of asking permission from the other person before doing anything to them; mandatory in any sexual situation. Minors cannot consent to sexual acts with adults.

Critical media literacy: The process through which we learn to evaluate different sources of media against each other, comparing how they cover the same issue, which perspectives they highlight, and what they may leave out; crucial for a functioning democratic society.

Cults: Small religious groups that are not part of a larger and more accepted religion, and that force their followers to believe things regarded by many people as extreme or dangerous.

Demisexual: Someone who experiences some sexual attraction, but only after forming a close emotional or romantic bond.

Depression: A mental health condition where someone feels sad more days than they're happy, and it's interfering with their ability to live their daily life; can be treated in lots of ways, including therapy and medication.

Derailing: Changing the subject instead of taking accountability.

Discrimination: When we take our prejudiced beliefs and put them into action, treating a person and/or group unfairly as a result.

Dyscalculia: A learning disability that impacts a person's ability to learn math skills and solve math problems; can be helped with certain strategies that lower anxiety about math and increase understanding about math terms and concepts.

Dyslexia: A learning disability that affects a person's reading, spelling, and pronunciation of sounds; can be helped with tutoring, listening to audiobooks as an alternative to reading, and typing on computers instead of writing by hand.

Dysphoria (gender): Feeling uncomfortable with your body because it doesn't match your gender and/or feeling discomfort after having a social interaction with someone who doesn't recognize—or outright disrespects—your gender identity. The opposite of this feeling is gender euphoria, when someone feels joy in expressing their authentic gender.

Ecosystem: A community of living things and the environment they live in. To understand ecosystems, it's important to know how plants, humans, and non-human animals are connected to each other and rely on each other for survival (interdependence).

Emotional maturity: Being able to understand and regulate our emotions, as well as communicate compassionately with others.

Environmental racism: When those in power disproportionately damage and pollute the environment in low-income communities of color, because they consider poor people of color's lives to be less valuable than the lives of wealthy white people.

Ethnicity: The cultural characteristics that make up a group of people in a geographic region, including their language, customs, music, ancestors, religion, and more.

Eugenics: A racist theory used by some scientists in the 1800s to pretend that white people were better than people of color.

Euphoria (gender): When someone feels joy in expressing their authentic gender.

Eurocentric beauty standards: Beauty standards that center European—usually white, Western European—bodily features.

Faith: Trusting that there's something good out there in the universe for us, despite what we're going through right now; can be the belief in something religious or non-religious.

Fatphobia: Discrimination against fat people; the fear and hatred of fatness.

Femicide: The murder of women and girls based on their gender.

Feminists: Activists for women's and girls' rights and gender equality.

Folk religions: Religions practiced by certain ethnic groups, tribes, and cultures in a specific geographic region outside organized religion. Many folk religions incorporate the idea of animism, the belief that everything around us (like animals, rocks, plants, and the weather) is alive and contains sacred energy.

Gay: Men who are sexually/romantically attracted mostly or exclusively to men. Sometimes women and non-binary people also use the word *gay* to describe themselves.

Gender affirmation treatments: A series of medical options that trans people may undergo to better align their bodies with their gender.

Gender binary: The outdated assumption that there are only two types of gender, male and female, which are dictated by our genitals; people will often use the gender binary to say there are "right ways" of being a girl or a boy, also known as gender norms.

Genes: The building blocks of our bodies' biological map for how tall, wide, hairy, short, light, dark, etc., we'll be based on the traits of our birth parents or their birth parents.

Genocide: When people in power kill, or attempt to kill, an entire population of people based on their race, nationality, ethnicity, sexuality, etc.

Gestational surrogate: Someone who agrees to carry a couple or single person's baby inside their body, gives birth to the baby, and gives the baby to the baby's parent(s) once the baby is born.

Global South: Africa, Latin America, parts of Oceania, and those parts of Asia and the Middle East most negatively impacted by global capitalism; usually low-income and with majority populations of people of color.

"Great both/and": The acknowledgment that we can feel seemingly very different emotions at the same time and it's all valid; a phrase coined by Sonya Renee Taylor.

Green flags: The opposite of red flags—things that feel good to us and our intuition, particularly in the context of a relationship.

Greysexual: Describes a person who typically experiences limited sexual attraction to others.

Haitian Revolution: When Haitians successfully rebelled in 1804 against French colonial rule of their country, becoming the first and only country to gain freedom from enslavement due to a national rebellion.

Health at Every Size (HAES) model: A health framework that says our size does not determine our health, and that people of all body types and sizes can practice healthy habits to take care of ourselves.

Heteronormativity: The unfair assumption that everyone is heterosexual, and that someone is heterosexual if they don't say otherwise. Also describes society's expectation that humans must follow traditional "male" and "female" gender roles.

Heterosexism: Prejudice and mistreatment that occurs when people unfairly think everyone is or should be heterosexual.

Heterosexual: A man who has sexual/romantic attraction primarily or exclusively to women, or a woman who has sexual/romantic attraction primarily or exclusively to men.

Hirsutism: A prominent development of female facial hair brought on by an underlying medical condition.

Homophobia: Hatred and discrimination against gay and lesbian people. Related forms of oppression include lesbophobia (discrimination against lesbians) and biphobia (discrimination against bisexual people). There has been a recent push by some to replace homophobia and similar terms ending in -phobia with the suffix -misia (so homophobia becomes homomisia) to focus on how discrimination and violence stem from beliefs of hatred rather than simple fear.

Hormones: Chemicals in your body that activate certain physical responses to help your body grow and thrive.

Hypervigilance: When our bodies are constantly on high alert because our nervous systems are waiting for the next bad thing to happen; stems from anxiety and trauma.

IEP (Individualized Education Program): A legal document for kids in US public schools that is customized to fit the unique educational needs of a specific child based on qualifying reasons, such as the child having ADHD or autism. IEPs are created by a team of helpers including school staff and the child's parent(s) or legal guardian(s).

Ifoga: A ritual in Samoan culture where someone who has done wrong covers themselves with a special mat in front of the house of the person they wronged to publicly apologize for what they or their family did. The whole village watches, and the person or family who has been wronged gets to decide whether they will accept the apology. Ifoga comes from the word *Ifo*, which means to bow down or lower oneself.

Incest: Sexual abuse that comes from a family member.

Interdependent: A relationship in which you each have your own lives as individual, unique people, but you also add to each other's lives as you go through life together. When describing a community, it's one in which our lives are connected, and we need each other to survive.

Interfaith dialogue: When people from different religious backgrounds come together to learn about each other's religious and spiritual traditions; usually results in a better appreciation for both the diversity of everyone's beliefs as well as the values that transcend their different faiths.

Internalized racism: When people of color end up thinking racist thoughts about our worth and value because of what our racist societies teach us from the time we're born.

Intersex: Those born with both male and female reproductive organs and other biological characteristics.

Intuition: The hard-to-describe sense we have in our bodies when we just know something; helps us determine what choices to make in life and in which direction we should go.

Islamophobia: Hatred and discrimination against Muslims.

Jim Crow: The system of local and state laws that white US Southerners passed in twenty-six states after the Civil War to make sure they could keep anti-Black racial discrimination legal (since they were no longer able to legally enslave Black people). This included segregation, which meant legally forcing Black people to attend separate (and not as well-funded) schools from white people, use separate drinking fountains, eat in separate restaurants, and more. These laws existed from the late 1800s until 1965.

Lesbian: Women who are sexually/romantically attracted mostly or exclusively to women.

LGBTQQIA2S+: An acronym of different identities within queer communities, including: lesbian, gay, bisexual, transgender, queer, questioning, intersex, asexual, two-spirit, and more.

Lobbyists: Groups with lots of money and political power who work to influence politicians by offering to give the politicians money if they vote the way the lobbyists want them to.

Love bombing: When someone gives another person lots of compliments, attention, and/or gifts to get that person to love and trust them, then starts acting in mean, cruel, and/or scary ways.

Mansplaining: When men explain things to women and people of other genders that they likely already know; occurs because of patriarchal societies making men think they're smarter and therefore authorities on all things.

Masturbation: Exploring by yourself what sexual sensations in your body you do and do not like.

Meditation: A practice that helps calm the mind and body by sitting quietly and focusing on the present moment.

Menopause: The time of life when a body that has experienced menstruation stops menstruating.

Menstrual cycle: The cycle from the day someone first sees menstrual blood until they see blood again the next month.

Monogamous: Referring to monogamy, the practice of two people in a romantic relationship deciding that they will only date each other and have no other romantic or sexual partners.

Mycelium: The vegetative part of a fungus, consisting of a network of fine white filaments (also called hyphae).

National identity: Someone's sense of who they are based on what country they're from.

Neurodiversity: The diverse ways in which our brains respond to the world around us and help us process information.

Non-binary: Someone who doesn't identify strictly as male or female.

Nuclear family: A family structure made up of a married mom and dad and their one or more children; often assumed to be the main family structure by our society and media when, in fact, there are many!

"One-drop rule": A racist policy adopted by pro-slavery US states that determined that any amount of Black blood made a person Black, thus making them eligible to be enslaved.

Organized religion: A term used to describe the churches, temples, and mosques many people grow up in, headed by religious leaders with specific texts and rules about what their members should and shouldn't do.

Pansexual: Someone who experiences sexual/romantic attraction to people regardless of their gender.

Parentification: Being forced to act as a parent to your caregiver instead of being able to act like their kid; can have long-term negative consequences, including developing depression and anxiety as an adult.

Patriarchy: A system of governance where men hold most of the power and women and other groups are significantly excluded from it; teaches everyone that women are weaker, less intelligent, and should be subservient to or beneath men.

Perfectionism: When someone wants to do well, to the point that they push themselves to be perfect and judge themself harshly when they don't live up to their own ultimately unattainable standards of perfection; tends to be linked to anxiety and stems from fear.

Period: The term many people use to informally describe the bodily experience of menstruation.

Philosophy: The study of how we understand nature, the world, and ourselves.

Polyamory: The practice of being in a romantic or sexual relation-ship with more than one person, with the knowledge and consent of all people involved.

Pornography: Sexually explicit media made for adults; illegal to show to young people under eighteen.

Prejudice: When we assume negative things about people without really knowing them.

Puberty: The time during which a young person's body begins to mature and becomes capable of reproducing.

Queer: An umbrella term for LGBTQQIA2S+ people, i.e., people who aren't both heterosexual and cisgender. Because the word queer started out as an anti-gay slur, not everyone in LGBTQQIA2S+ communities use it, and some think that it should remain a word that only queer people have the right to reclaim and use.

Racism: The combination of racial prejudice plus power, which results in racial discrimination.

Radical self-love: The inner remembering that you are already enough and worthy, already amazing just as you are—because you EXIST on this planet in this time and space, and come from the love of the universe; a term coined by Sonya Renee Taylor.

Reciprocity: The idea that relationships shouldn't be one-sided; both people should put in effort to make it work.

Red flags: Things that don't seem quite right and are warning us to be careful, or even stop; in a relationship, signs that there's a problem or that you may be in an abusive relationship.

Religious pluralism: Having a basic respect for other religions so that people from different religious backgrounds can live together peacefully in society.

Reparations: Monetary payments to take accountability for having done harm or damage.

"Reverse racism": The faulty argument that pointing out racism is itself racist, usually to downplay the reality of racism. Reverse racism isn't possible, since prejudice against white people isn't built into systems and structures of power.

Right relationship: A term with roots in many cultural traditions around the world, and used in this book to describe the act of honoring each person's dignity and seeing them as valuable and worthy just for existing; also describes doing our part to fix the systems of oppression that were built before we as humans understood our radical self-love.

Sexism: Prejudice and discrimination based on the belief that the male sex is superior.

Speciesism: The belief that humans matter more than all the other species on our planet.

Spirituality: The belief in a higher power, deity or deities, or reverence for the universe, but in a way that allows people the flexibility to choose for themselves what beliefs make the most sense to them. Can involve having certain religious beliefs without following an organized religion, or believing in some things from one religion and some things from another.

Stewardship: The job of supervising or taking care of something; is often used to talk about protecting the environment.

STI: Sexually transmitted infection.

Stonewall Uprising: The riots that took place in New York City in June 1969 by members of trans, lesbian, and gay communities in response to homophobic and transphobic police brutality at the Stonewall Inn; one of the history-changing events that sparked the modern-day gay rights movement.

Suicide: The act of killing yourself; when someone has thoughts about killing themselves (whether they take action to do so or not), they are considered suicidal.

Toxic masculinity: A type of sexist masculinity often encouraged in society, where boys and men are told by their culture that violence is the best and only way to deal with their emotions or solve their problems.

Transgender: A person whose gender does not correspond with the sex they were assigned at birth; often shortened to "trans."

Transphobia: Fear of, and hatred against, transgender people.

Trauma: Upsetting things we've gone through in life that still affect our actions or decisions, whether we're aware of it or not.

Two-spirit: A term used in certain Indigenous communities since the early 1990s to refer to Indigenous people of diverse gender roles and sexualities, such as people who were understood to have both male and female spirits inside themselves, and who were considered sacred by their communities; many different tribes have their own words in their own languages for this general concept, which has existed since before white people colonized North America.

Undocumented: When referring to immigrants, someone who has immigrated to a country without having completed the legal process to do so; a few reasons for immigrating without documentation include fleeing violence, not being able to afford the legal process, and fleeing as a child with your caregiver(s).

United Nations (UN): A collection of countries—originally 51 countries when it was founded in 1945 after World War II, but now made up of 193 countries (almost every country on earth)—whose governments agreed they would meet to try to prevent and stop wars using only peaceful methods. Some other issues the UN focuses on include promoting human rights, helping refugees, and protecting the environment. In practice, the UN often faces international criticism for not accomplishing its goals.

Universal Basic Income: A sum of money provided to all citizens of a country, regardless of their employment status or income. It is a way to minimize poverty in countries by making sure every citizen has some money to take care of their basic needs.

Vaginal Discharge: Fluid or mucus that keeps your vagina clean and moist and protects it from infection. It is normally white or clear and has minimal smell.

Vegans: People who don't eat any animal products (such as meat, dairy, and honey).

Vegetarians: People who don't eat meat.

Western countries: Nations that have been culturally, politically, and economically shaped by European values and ideas.

Whiteness: The outcome of different groups of Europeans, who had previously fought amongst each other and argued over religion, land, and power, uniting as white and declaring their false superiority over people of color in order to gain power over them. Believed to have been created in big part to justify enslaving people of color.

White privilege: The unearned advantages white people have access to just by being born white in a racist society; ensures the challenges white people have will not be because of their racial identity.

White supremacist delusion: A term coined by Sonya Renee Taylor to describe the false belief that whiteness is best, often used to justify racism and white violence.

Xenophobia: Fear of and hatred against people considered "foreign."

RESOURCES

Adios Barbie: adiosbarbie.com

African Queer Youth Initiative: aqyi.org/

Ahwaa: majal.org/ahwaa

AMAZE: amaze.org

Asexuality Visibility and Education Network (AVEN): asexuality.org

Barnow, Rev. Blyth: femminary.com/about/

Bastida, Xiye: www.xiyebeara.com/

The Body Is Not an Apology: thebodyisnotanapology.com

Bornstein, Kate: katebornstein.com/

Bowers, Dr. Marci: marcibowers.com

CDC LGBT Youth Resources: cdc.gov/lgbthealth/youth-resources.htm

Center for Body Trust: centerforbodytrust.com/

Childhelp: 1.800.422.4453; childhelp.org

Copeny, Mari ("Little Miss Flint"): maricopeny.com/

Crabbe, Megan: bodyposipanda.com/

Futures Without Violence: futureswithoutviolence.org/

GLAAD: glaad.org

GLSEN: glsen.org; also glsen.org/supporting-trans-and-gnc-students

Gualinga, Helena: oneearth.org/climate-hero-helena-gualinga/

Health at Every Size: asdah.org/health-at-every-size-haes-approach/

Hirsi, Isra: internationalcongressofyouthvoices.com/isra-hirsi

The International Lesbian, Gay, Bisexual, Transgender, Queer, and Intersex Youth and Student Organisation (IGLYO): iglyo.com

"Introduction to Media Literacy: Crash Course Media Literacy #1": youtube.com/watch?v=AD7N-1Mj-DU

Jones, Kimberley Latrice: kimjoneswrites.com/about

LANDBACK movement: landback.org/

Le Refuge (France): le-refuge.org/

LGBT Youth Line (Canada): 1.800.268.9688 (phone); 647.694.4275 (text); youthline.ca/

LGBT Youth Scotland: lgbtyouth.org.uk/

McIntosh, Peggy, "The Invisible Knapsack of White Privilege": nationalseedproject.org/Key-SEED-Texts/white-privilege -unpacking-the-invisible-knapsack

Minus18 (Australia): minus18.org.au/

The Movement for Black Lives: m4bl.org/

Movimiento Cosecha: lahuelga.com/

National Center for Transgender Equality's Youth & Students page: transequality.org/issues/youth-students

Peltier, Autumn: cnn.com/2022/08/09/americas/autumn -peltier-water-protector-first-nations-canada-spc/index.html

Planned Parenthood: plannedparenthood.org/

Pride House Tokyo: pridehouse.jp/en/about/

"Poodle Science": youtube.com/watch?v=H89QQfXtc-k

RainbowYOUTH (Aotearoa / New Zealand): ry.org.nz/about-us

Rodriguez, Bruno: climatehub.nytimes.com/speaker/358597 /bruno-rodr%C3%ADguez

Rupert, Dr. Loucresie: insightfulconsultant.org/about/

Sunrise Movement: sunrisemovement.org/

Sylvia Rivera Law Project: srlp.org/

Taylor, Sonya Renee. *Celebrate Your Body (and Its Changes, Too!): The Ultimate Puberty Book for Girls.* sonyareneetaylor .com/books/celebrate-your-body-and-its-changes-too-the -ultimate-puberty-book-for-girls

Them: them.us

Thunberg, Greta: fridaysforfuture.org/what-we-do/who-we-are/

Transgender Law Center's Youth Resources page: transgenderlawcenter.org/resources/youth

Trans Lifeline: translifeline.org/

The Trevor Project: thetrevorproject.org

Vaid-Menon, Alok: alokvmenon.com/

Voices of Youth: voicesofyouth.org/

Weber, Dr. Shannon: shannonweberphd.com/

Yeboah, Stephanie: stephanieyeboah.com/

Young Voices for the Planet: youngvoicesfortheplanet.com/

Yousafzai, Malala: malala.org/malalas-story?sc=header

ABOUT OUR EXPERTS

Minster Blyth Barnow (she/her) is a queer, white, Christian femme, living in Ohio. She is a preacher, harm reductionist, writer, and community organizer. Blyth founded Femminary to offer spiritual care for communities "the church" has excluded and harmed, including queers, people who use drugs, sex workers, working class people, and organizers. She loves putting bow ties on her dog Birdy, finding new recipes for cabbage, and creating sacred rituals for others. Her writing also appears in *Beyond Survival: Strategies and Stories from the Transformative Justice Movement* (edited by Ejeris Dixon and Leah Lakshmi Piepzna-Samarasinha) and *The Care We Dream Of: Liberatory and Transformative Approaches to LGBTQ+ Health* by Zena Sharman.

Kate Bornstein (they/them, she/her) is an author, actor, and performance artist. For over thirty years, she has been writing award-winning books on the subject of non-binary gender. Kate maintains a career in theater, having made her Broadway debut in the summer of 2018, co-starring in the Second Stage Theater's production of Young Jean Lee's *Straight White Men*. Kate's 2006 book, *Hello, Cruel World: 101 Alternatives to Suicide for Teens, Freaks, and Other Outlaws* propelled Kate into an international position of advocacy for marginalized youth, for which she has earned two citations of honor from the New York City Council.

Keah Brown (she/her) is an award-winning journalist, author, studying actress, and screenwriter. She is the recipient of Ulta Beauty's Muse 100 award, which is a celebration of 100 inspirational voices around beauty. She is also one of The Root's 100 most influential African Americans of 2018. Keah is the creator of the viral hashtag #DisabledAndCute. Her work on disability, identity, and pop culture has appeared in *Town & Country*, *Teen Vogue*, *Elle*, *Harper's Bazaar*, *Marie Claire UK*, and *The New York Times*, among other publications. Her essay collection *The Pretty One* and picture book *Sam's Super Seats* are out now. Forthcoming is a young adult novel titled *The Secret Summer Promise*. Find out more at keahbrown.com

Jeanne Greene (she/her) is a mother, dancer, fantastic cook, wife, and shopping aficionado. She is also an adoptee who reconnected with her birth family in 1998. Jeanne spent many years fiercely advocating for educational support for her autistic son and loves jewelry making and spending time with her loved ones. She resides in western Pennsylvania.

Kimberly Latrice Jones (she/her) is an American author and filmmaker. She is known for the *New York Times* bestselling young adult novel *I'm Not Dying With You Tonight*, co-authored with Gilly Segal, and the viral video "How Can We Win," published during the George Floyd protests. *I'm Not Dying With You Tonight* was nominated for an NAACP Image award, Georgia Author Of The Year award, and the Cybils Awards, and was also selected as the September 2019 book club pick for the Barnes & Noble YA book club and Overdrive's Big Library Read. From her viral video came the inspiration for her subsequent book *How We Can Win: Race, History and Changing the Money Game That's Rigged.* Kimberly resides in Atlanta and is the proud mother of a gifted boy.

Loucresie Rupert, MD (she/her) is a psychiatrist treating children, adolescents, and adults who currently practices at Gundersen Health System. She specializes in neurodiversity (ADHD, autism, learning differences, etc.), children with trauma, children in foster care or who have been adopted, and adults with developmental disabilities. She currently aids in the fight toward racial, sexual orientation, gender identity, religious, areligious, disability, and neurodiverse equality through her work as co-founder of Physician Women SOAR (Support, Organize, Advocate, Reclaim), an organization of physician women that raises money and awareness and educates for the aforementioned intersectional causes. Loucresie also serves her community through her participation in B.L.A.C.K. (Black Leaders Acquiring Collective Knowledge). She aims to help empower those with mental health diagnoses and neurodiversity through her company, Insightful Consultant LLC, via speaking engagements, education, and training on a plethora of mental health and diversity-related topics.

Dr. Shannon Weber (she/her) is the Director of Digital Learning at the global digital media and education company The Body Is Not An Apology, founded by Sonya Renee Taylor. Shannon is also the author of three books on social justice, most recently the children's book *Activists Assemble: We Are All Equal!* She holds a PhD in Feminist Studies and previously taught gender studies and sociology courses at a handful of top colleges and universities in California and Massachusetts, including Tufts University and Brandeis University. Born in Los Angeles, Shannon was raised in the Northwest and has lived on both the East and West Coasts of the US as an adult. She currently resides in New England with her partner, dog Francesca, and cat Olivia.

ACKNOWLEDGMENTS

This book was a surprising challenge to complete. Not only was I writing in a pandemic lockdown and complete isolation, but I also love young people so much and had much fear that I might "get it wrong" or "mess up." Things little Sonya has always worried about. Thank goodness I had such amazing people helping me bring this book into the world.

I want to thank my agent Monica Odom, who believed in this project from the beginning but more importantly, believed in me. I also want to thank my editor Nancy Mercado, who felt like I had something important to share with young people, invited me to do so, and allowed me the space and time for this project to come together authentically. I would also like to thank Rosie Ahmed, whose guidance and suggestions ensured this book was the best it could be.

My teammate and brilliant Director of Digital Learning, Shannon Weber, is a magician whose attention to details and rigor made this book more than just my thoughts and ideas, but instead a powerful, well-researched asset for young people. Additionally, I would like to extend a huge thanks to Advocates for Youth, who helped organize listening sessions with the youth in their programs. Those sessions assisted in shaping the foundation of this project.

Most importantly, I want to thank the many young people from around the world who trusted me enough to submit their honest, vulnerable, silly, scary, profound, brilliant questions and allowed me to share my reflections and resources with them in turn. What a gift you all are, and how immensely hopeful I feel knowing the future lies with you.

Lucky me. Lucky all of us. Thank you for being amazing.